THE DOVECOTES OF TINOS
Strolling through the craft of stonemasonry in 1955

The entire corpus of this study was donated in 2021 by the architects Manuel and Aristea Baud-Bovy to the Archive of Modern Greek Architecture in Benaki Museum, so that it may become accessible to researchers and scholars.

© KAPON EDITIONS, 2021
ISBN 978-618-5209-81-0

All rights reserved under law 2387/20 (modified under law 2121/93 which is in effect today) and under the Bern Convention (ratified under law 100/1975). This book or parts thereof may not be reproduced in any form, stored in any retrieval system, or transmitted in any form by any means — electronic, mechanical, photocopy, recording, or otherwise — without prior written permission of the publisher.

KAPON EDITIONS
23–27 Makriyanni str., 117 42 Athens, Greece, Tel. 0030 210 9235098
RACHEL'S BOOKSHOP
22 Ploutarchou str., 106 76 Athens, Greece, Tel. 0030 210 9210983
www.kaponeditions.gr   e-mail: info@kaponeditions.gr

Manuel Baud-Bovy

THE DOVECOTES OF TINOS

Strolling through the craft of stonemasonry in 1955

TRANSLATED BY: **Dr DONIERT EVELY**

KAPON EDITIONS

CONTENTS

INTRODUCTION YANNIS CH. PAPAIOANNOU	6
TWO TRAVELLERS IN TINOS IN 1919	8
FOREWORD	11
GENERAL DESCRIPTION	
The island of the dovecotes	12
When were the dovecotes built?	13
Is their origin venetian… or local?	14
The main elements of a dovecote	16
The rules for positioning and construction	18
The structure of the walls	20
The method of roofing	22
The elements of the crowning of the dovecotes	25
The composition of the decoration	28
The origin of the decorative motifs	30
The transformations of the cypress tree	32
The variations on the sun motif	34
From the limitations of folk architecture…	36
… to the creation of a style	37
THE MAP OF THE ISLAND	38
FIRST ROUTE West coast: from Kionia to Ktikados, Hatzirados, Tarambados and Kardiani	41
SECOND ROUTE Northwest part of the island: Exo Meri and Kato Meri	99
THIRD ROUTE From the plateau of Steni to the town of Tinos and the southeast part of the island	139

These dovecotes, amongst the most beautiful on the island, are located above Tarambados (17, 18, 21) (photo by M. Kapon).

INTRODUCTION

Amongst the treasures of traditional Cycladic architecture, alongside the houses and the churches, there is a rich range of agricultural buildings, such as dovecotes and windmills. In all his work, the folk craftsman harmonizes utilitarian needs with an innate elegance and ingenuity, always keeping matters in proportion and respecting not only the local conditions but also the dictates of the natural environment. Dovecotes, scattered on the hillsides of other islands too like Andros, Mykonos and Sifnos, are a representative and almost emblematic part of the architecture of the Aegean archipelago. But nowhere can match the incomparable wealth and variety of those on Tinos —known in antiquity as *Hydroussa*, fond of the water, due to its abundance of springs— home of so many famous artisans. It is believed that the care of and interest in pigeons began during the Venetian occupation with the privileged right to possess a dovecote, although the first document for such a building dates back only to 1726, a time when the period of Ottoman rule had just begun. A dovecote was not only something of value and worth, but ownership of one was also a declaration of noble origin, so that over the years these buildings and their delicate decoration which can be described as "embroidery in stone", became established as symbols of the economic and social status of the owner.

The dove, the sacred bird of Aphrodite, once an erotic symbol and later the incarnation of the Holy Spirit, timeless harbinger of peace —but also a generous provider of food and fertilizer— has been fittingly honoured in many far-flung regions of the world.

However, neither the dovecotes of Western Europe (in Scotland, England, France, Spain and Italy) nor those of the Islamic world (Iran, Qatar, Egypt and Sudan) have much in common in their shape or appearance with these masterpieces of the Aegean islands.

On the occasion of the book you are holding in your hands, I have the pleasure of presenting the author's particular background and origins: the person who in the very nick of time (in 1955) completed his endeavour to rescue the Tenian dovecotes, is more than just an inspired architect and philhellene scholar.

His initiative to literally roam all over the island, capturing its most representative architectural treasure at a time when no one else had even thought of such a thing, is paired with a rare third generation creative DNA.

In 1913, his grandfather, Daniel Baud-Bovy, director of the Geneva School of Fine Arts, was the first to reach the summit of Mount Olympus, while in 1919 he published (with photographs by Fred Boissonas) the iconic book *From the Cyclades to Crete at the Behest of the Wind*.

In 1929, his father, Samuel Baud-Bovy, a leading ethnomusicologist and ardent Hellenist, came to Greece and wrote his dissertation on the *Songs of the Dodecanese*, a tradition then under Italian occupation. Later on, he preserved and recorded musical treasures of Epirus, Thessaly, Thessaloniki and Crete. Thus, the arrival of the young Architecture student, Manuel Baud-Bovy, in Tinos in 1955, occurred just before the impact of the new economic conditions that would open the floodgates of mass tourism and the inevitable commercialization of everything. As bearer of this cultural legacy, and imbued with maintaining his philhellenic education, Manuel Baud-Bovy came to study and in fact to save these "embroideries in stone", which are so in harmony with the landscape of the Cyclades. The detection, organization, recording and documentation of this material, combined with a remarkable ability to observe and a unique artistic sensitivity (let's not forget that his great-grandfather was also a well-known painter), brought to completion the painstaking rescue research in a relatively short time.

Today, when the various places and sites of the island have become more easily accessible, and when the possibilities afforded to a photographer by technological means make it all more like child's-play, the physical wear and the enormous efforts required back in 1955 are not readily grasped. It is also noticeable that in the years that have elapsed —that brought us from walking the fields to flying over them with a drone— many such monuments have been lost in the inevitable ravages of time. The author of this book, a French-speaking Swiss, has been moved by the passion that seizes the true lovers of Greece. He has a deep sense of the *genius loci*, its relationship with the light, and of the zeal of the folk craftsmen. As an experienced architect, he knows that the relationship of an edifice to its surroundings and landscape is reflected in its particular features and form, as well as in the way it serves the needs of everyday life. He also understands that aesthetics presupposes a moral attitude towards Mother Nature and her creations.

I recall excerpts from the *Greek Summer* of Jacques Lacarrière, and I find parallels between the divinely inspired mood of that young Frenchman of the 1950s, and the creative inspiration that moved today's honouree. Orator Isocrates, addressing his Athenian fellow citizens, had said that "Greeks are those who share in our education" (*Panegyricus* 50). I will paraphrase that sentiment here, by including the Muses Marguerite Yourcenar and Jacqueline de Romilly, and I will say that "Greeks are those who share in the philhellenic education".

I will go further still: Manuel Baud-Bovy excelled doubly, in choosing as his life partner and collaborator the eminent Greek architect and urban planner Aristea Tzanou. Always by her side, he donated the whole of his grandfather's documents to the Thessaloniki Museum of Photography in 2013. The dovecotes of Tinos already share an extensive bibliography and the surviving examples have been systematically photographed and recorded. At the end of the book is an indicative sample of the most accessible bibliography. However, the extensive 1955 tour of these masterpieces of the stone-worker's craft consists a corpus, revealing more as one delves ever deeper. It is not just its value as a great architectural travelogue, geographically divided into three routes. It is a clear and systematic scientific study, a penetrating scrutiny of the typology, structure and decorative merits of these idiosyncratic agricultural constructions. A plain but comprehensive record of 87 selected examples enhanced by a well-documented testimony with plans of impressive completeness and clarity. The work of then a young man, who today as a hale and hearty elder accepts his lively book as a gift in return.

I believe that the trustworthy meeting of this monograph with the couple of Moses and Rachel Kapon was due to some stellar synergy. I do not know if it was the particular affinities the two couples had with their beloved Pelion, or the common passion they share for achieving the best possible result. But I do know that the work is done with love, with an eye for those who will appreciate and treasure it. After some forty years of friendship and an equal experience of collaboration with Rachel and Moses Kapon (and having personally met important scholarly authors), let me share my own happiness in being associated —even in the small way that I am — with this unique edition.

YANNIS CH. PAPAIOANNOU
Architect, National Technical University of Athens

TWO TRAVELLERS IN TINOS IN 1919

In 1919, two travellers involved in writing the book *Des Cyclades en Crète au gré du vent*, found themselves in Tinos and were impressed by the dovecotes they saw.

Daniel Baud-Bovy dedicated three pages to them: "In every corner there stand small, peculiar buildings, very pleasant to look at. They have strange ramparts on their roofs. Slate slabs —arranged in rectangular shapes, one on top of the other, in triangles, in zig-zag garlands— pierce their facades and look, from afar, like stretched-out lace. At first glance, these small buildings bring to mind some turrets of the Italian Renaissance which alter the physiognomy of the landscape. White palaces, elegantly carved, to match their inhabitants: the cooing pigeons.

The Venetian nobles who ruled the island in the 18th century, established, among other feudal privileges, the *droit de colombier* (the dovecote right), that Jacques Bonhomme found hard to accept.[1] They raised up the dovecotes, which are still in operation. In Naxos, for example, which was also a Venetian duchy, the birds housed in the cotes, were exported in barrels, preserved in vinegar. In Tinos, however, there are more dovecotes than anywhere else, and they lend the island a special aura."

---

1. "Jacques Bonhomme" was a name given to the peasants that revolted in 14th c. France against the privileges of nobility, which included the dovecote right, after the leader of the revolted, Jacques Bonhomme.

I. During his visit in 1919, the photographer Fred Boissonas took many photographs, including that of a dovecote in the village of Kionia (1), in its original condition. Baud-Bovy's image of 1955 (see pp. 48–49) reveals the changes made to the facades.

FOREWORD

My father's friends, Gustave and Cyrille Dorier, built the first cottage on the beach of Kionia, including a small dovecote. At that time, they were still roaming there from the port of Tinos on foot. In the summer of 1955, I was invited on vacation to accompany their son, Jean-Marc, who was a little younger than me.

Going up to one of the nearby villages, I discovered these strange buildings, about which I had heard nothing. I remember the surprise and admiration I felt when, on each of my trips, I discovered on deserted sandy beaches or lying on hillsides, imposing dovecotes, each one more beautiful than the last.

From this visit to Tinos I can still recall the variety of landscapes and the hospitality offered to me by the villagers everywhere I went. I remember the *cafenion*-owner of a small village who offered me shelter for the night, the festival in Ysternia… where some people wanted to bring a priest and marry me, the old man who insisted I drink his miraculous water to cure my myopia.

I had decided to undertake a systematic recording of the dovecotes. For two months, I crisscrossed the whole island, sometimes on foot and sometimes on a mule, because cars were scarce then. Sometimes I slept in a village and sometimes under the stars, on a threshing floor, in a chapel or even in an abandoned dovecote. I discovered around eight hundred of them. My drawings, descriptions and questions filled four large albums, which I presented at the Geneva School of Architecture where I was studying.

About sixty years later, I had the opportunity to show my work to the publishers Moses and Rachel Kapon. They were interested in my work and decided to publish a concise version of it. I would like to express my gratitude for their generosity, patience and special care for this demanding editorial task.

Thanks to them, there will be a testimony left of the exceptional dovecotes of Tinos, at a time when many of them have already disappeared, or they have been reduced to ruins. I would also like to express my sincere gratitude to architect Dr Yiannis Papaioannou who wrote the introduction and edited my text.

May this book encourage and inspire the inhabitants of Tinos who are trying to preserve this memory of their past!

MANUEL BAUD-BOVY, Architect

2. It is very rare to walk the terrain of Tinos and not meet, between terraces and lush vegetation, an unusual dovecote (photo by M. Kapon).

THE ISLAND OF THE DOVECOTES

In Tinos, dovecotes can be seen everywhere:
The most beautiful can be found isolated in gardens, near a village or a little further away or near a spring that irrigates a garden. Others, in the middle of a field, amidst the fig and olive groves, are often associated with a wine press or a threshing floor for wheat. Sometimes, in the village, a dovecote is built into the corner of a house.
Usually, however, the dovecote is far from the village and almost always includes a room on the ground floor, where the owner can store his tools and the harvest, and possibly spend the night. The dovecote then turns into a "hut".
Thanks to its innumerable springs (which gave it the name of *Hydrousa* in antiquity), Tinos is one of the most cultivated islands of the Cyclades: from the sea-shore and almost to the very mountain peaks, the old inhabitants turned the slopes into stepped fields, where they cultivated wheat, olives, figs and vines. As a matter of fact, a few mulberries from the old silk industry live on.
The abundance of springs and the spread of crops throughout almost the entire island (197 sq. km), explain the equally wide dispersal of dovecotes throughout Tinos.
Moreover, the dovecotes of Tinos are undoubtedly the most beautiful and the most numerous in the Cyclades. We still may meet many in Andros or, more rarely, in Mykonos, Syros or Naxos, but they look like pale imitations of the Tenian prototypes. Even if we accept, then, that it was the Tenian model that spread to the neighbouring islands, the question of *its* origin still remains.

3

3–4. Dovecotes can be found all over the island, near a village (Hatzirados), or in an isolated area. Many of them rise in abrupt slopes while others are to be found amidst idyllic valleys and gently stepped hills, often in close vicinity to each other.

WHEN WERE THE DOVECOTES BUILT?

Most were built in the first half of the 20th century. Building was still going on when I was on the island, in the 1950s. Many date from the first half of the 19th century, and even more from the middle or late parts of the same century.
As far as I know, only one dovecote, in Tarambados, dates from the 18th century: a marble slab states that the house to which it belonged was built in 1745. Judging by their style, there is no doubt that other dovecotes, albeit relatively few, date as well from this time or a little earlier. But none seems to be very much older.

To conclude, then, were any dovecotes built in Tinos before the end of the 18th century? Maybe. However, some older structures may have collapsed in the meantime.
Are there any texts that can inform us? Neither Dapper, Spon, or Wheller, nor Tournefort, nor Choiseul-Gouffier mention dovecotes in their travel narratives, although they have existed ever since. A reference is made only at the beginning of the 20th century, in Markos Zallony's book, *Voyage à Tine*: "Almost all the inhabitants have one dovecote, and so, all year round, they eat many pigeons."

IS THEIR ORIGIN VENETIAN...

This is a possibility often mentioned. Indeed, Tinos was one of the duchies that Venice kept under its power for a very long time, from 1207 until the Ottoman invasion in 1715. This long occupation explains the fact that one third of the island's inhabitants are Catholics. But what are the arguments for the Venetian origin of the Tenian dovecote?
- Dovecotes are usually found on Greek islands that were Venetian duchies. Not, however, in all the Greek islands occupied by the Venetians.
- There were dovecotes all over Italy, mainly until 1789, when the *droit de colombier* was abolished. They have, however, a very different form: they are tall circular towers, but little decorated.
- The nomenclature of the various parts of the dovecote includes many terms of Italian origin: the words for column, bench, parapet, door, embellishments, etc. However, most of these terms are often used in the Greek language, even in areas where dovecotes are unknown.
- Old dovecotes are extremely rare on the Exo Meri, where Venetian influence was minimal. On the contrary, in Orthodox areas, such as Triantaros, Arnados, Duo Choria or Berdemiaros, there are many old examples.

... OR LOCAL?

A Venetian origin has not been proven. After all, the Tenian dovecote does not look like its counterpart in Europe or the Middle East, such as in Egypt or Iran. So, is the dovecote of Tinos a local development?

The ancient Greeks knew of pigeons; they used them as messengers. Varro, in *De re rustica*, prefers a Greek term (περιστερεών, pigeonary or pigeon-farm) instead of the Latin term *columbarium*; this is an indication of the importance of dovecotes in ancient Greece.

We cannot rule out the possibility that dovecotes have been in Tinos from antiquity to the present day: the springs and crops of the island are favourable factors. The fact that everywhere in Tinos thin slate slabs or marble are to be found, perhaps explains their oh-so characteristic decoration.

5. The second dovecote that Fred Boissonas mentions in his book. It is built of local stone, though not from the steep cliff-face that rises behind it. The *liastres*, the nesting-niches, the slate rhombi of the austere decoration can be clearly seen, and on the roof the corner columns with a big banquette in between them.

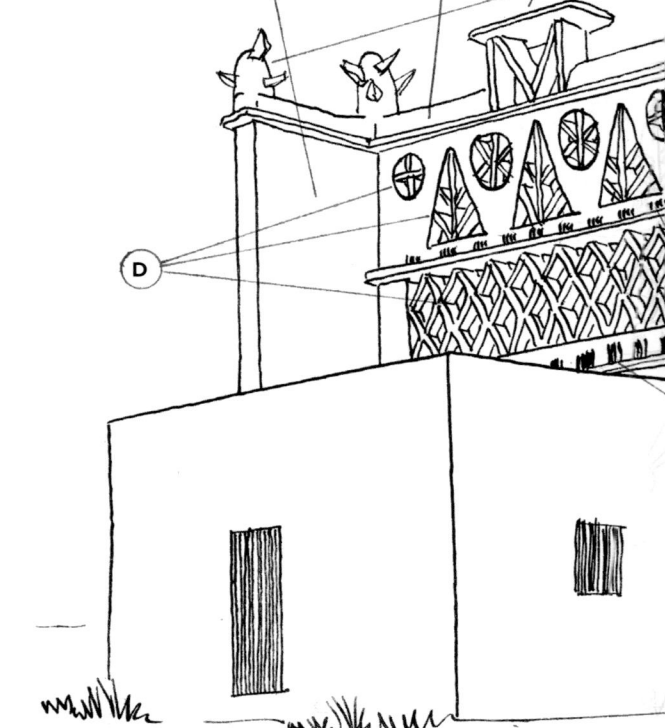

THE MAIN ELEMENTS OF A DOVECOTE

There are two main categories
I. In the first category ("dovecote-hut"), the ground floor is larger than the first floor, or one of its front sides might extend to the side. The pigeons are usually confined to the first floor.
II. In the second category, usually near a village, the dovecotes consist of a single, relatively tall building, which sometimes takes the form of a tower, with a square or L-shape form at the ground level.

The elements that make up the Tenian dovecote are the following:
1. The ground-floor, with or without external extension, usually with door and windows.
2. A protruding anta wall, commonly called *magoulo* (cheek) **(M)**, decorated or not, that shelters the dovecote from the wind.

3. One or more horizontally decorative friezes, consisting of:
• A continuous series of small projecting slabs, commonly called *liastres* **(L)**, allowing the pigeon to land more easily at the entrance to the small openings.
• A series of small openings **(O)**, which run right through the wall from face to face, allowing the pigeons to enter.
• A decoration **(D)**, comprising many small niches of various shapes, made up of narrow slabs.

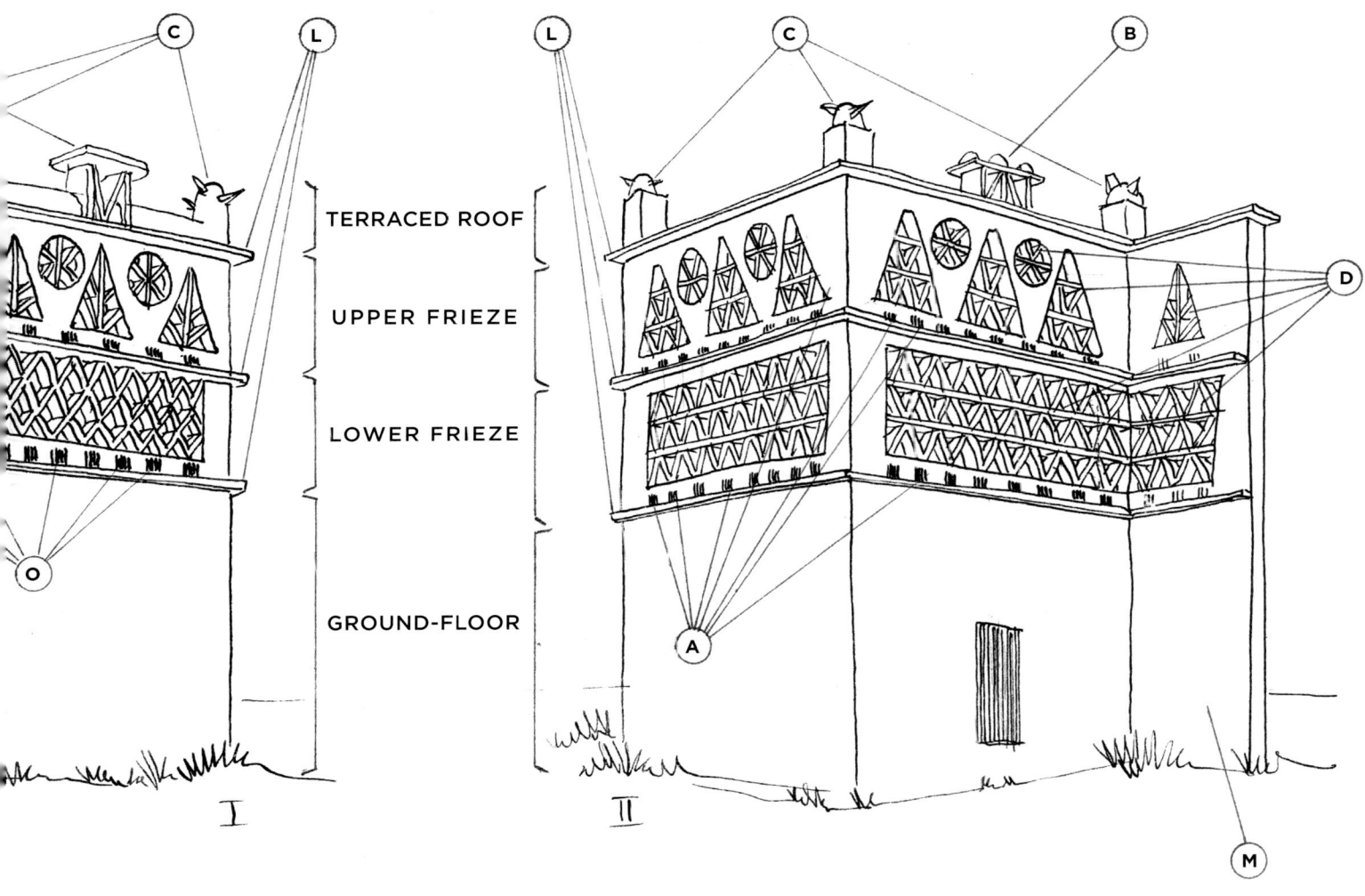

4. The crowning of the building, which consists of:
• A small wall **(W)** that surrounds the terraced roof.
• Small columns **(C)** at the corners.
• One or more "banquettes" (benches) **(B)** in the centre of the facades, decorative elements where the pigeons can rest. Inside there are the nests (measuring 20×20×20 cm), where the pigeons lay their eggs. The owner collects from these nests the squabs that are intended for cooking. Gone are the days (in the early 20th century) when pigeons were exported "in barrels preserved in vinegar" (D. Baud-Bovy, *Des Cyclades en Crète au gré du vent*, Geneva 1919, p. 30).

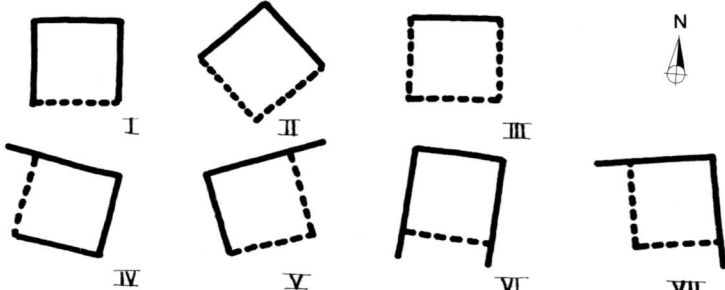

THE RULES FOR POSITIONING AND CONSTRUCTION

The erection of a dovecote must meet three criteria:
• The dovecotes must be adapted to the orientation of the terraces on the slopes: one facade will always be parallel to the buttresses supporting the terrace
• Construction of small openings allowing access to the pigeons on the facade that faces the slope.
• Protection of the facades facing north. Dovecotes usually have one or two decorated facades, with small openings. Theoretically, when there is only one such facade, it is oriented to the south (I). When there are two facades, they are oriented to the southeast and southwest (II). I saw only two or three dovecotes with three such orientations (III). It can happen, however, that a dovecote has a facade partially facing north. This disadvantage is compensated by projecting anta-walls or *magoula* ("cheeks") (IV to VII).

The *magoula* can cover a facade to its entire height or rise to just above the ground floor of the dovecote. Their cornice is, in general, similar to that of the dovecote itself. A small column usually rises at their edges. In some cases, the decoration of the main facade continues up to the corner of the wall, and then runs on onto the *magoulo* itself, without any change.

6. In order to shelter the building from the north wind, the facades of the dovecotes facing north have no openings at all. This particular building is oriented to the south and the sea. Its owner can be seen together with his draught animals on the threshing floor, trampling his wheat to separate the grains.

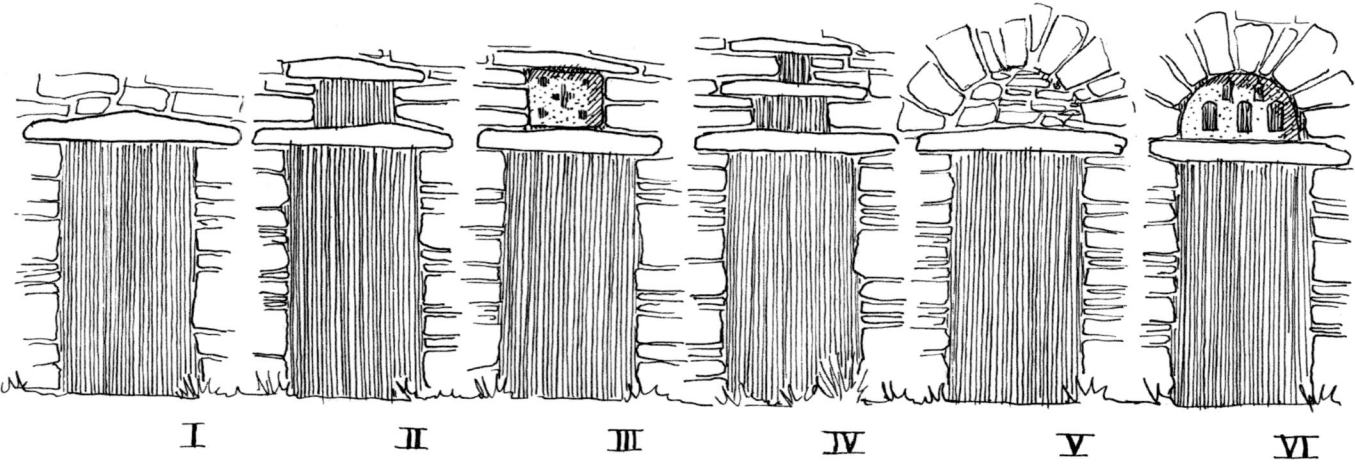

THE STRUCTURE OF THE WALLS

The native bedrock of the island consists of slates and, in places, solid masses of marble. Slate was usually used to build the walls. In general, the walls are 60 cm thick, but usually their thickness varies, tapering from 90 cm at the base to 50 cm at the top. They used to bind the masonry with a mortar of raw soil mixed with water, sometimes reinforced with lime, and recently with cement.

The small openings intended for the entrance of the pigeons are usually 10 to 12 cm wide and 10 to 15 cm high. If they were larger, various predators would be able to get inside the dovecote. The openings are set 15 to 30 cm apart and rest on a protruding slab (the *liastra*), where the pigeons can rest.

Inside the dovecote, nesting boxes are made where pigeons can brood. These take the form of niches, a cube with a side of 20 to 30 cm, distributed in various places, as in the corners of the dovecote. Their number varies greatly, from 20 to 200, depending on the size of the dovecote.

Doors and windows usually widen to the interior. They are topped by a stone lintel (I), and exceptionally with a few pieces of wood. There are many ways to lessen the load carried by the lintel: by employing two or three lintels (II to IV), by using relief arches, the opening of which is filled with masonry (V), or blocked by a slat or marble slab, usually carved (VI).

7. A characteristic example of a dovecote built on the edge of a step rock (77), belonging to Kardamitzis family from Triantaros (drawing in p. 163)

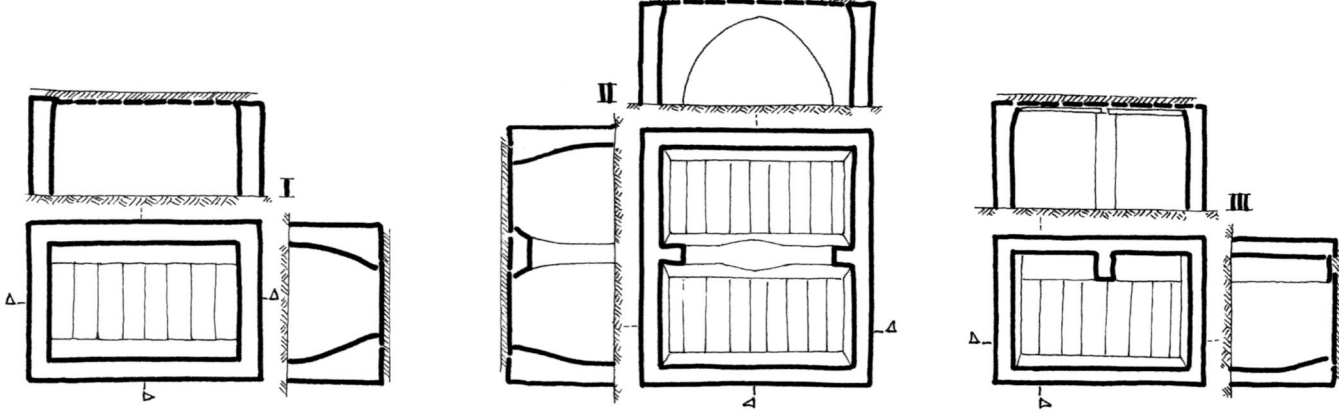

THE METHOD OF ROOFING

Almost all dovecotes are covered with a flat, terraced roof. Waterproofing is achieved with a final top layer of clayey soil (compacted with a marble roller every year, when the first rains fall), or with a layer of plaster-mortar, consisting of gravel, sand and lime, sometimes even a little cement. Usually, the roofing itself is made from irregular or squared wooden joist-beams, which in the latest dovecotes are replaced with ones of iron. Very often, however, the roof is supported by slate slabs, whose length reaches and can even exceed two meters. They are always well shaped, so that they are firmly joined to each other, on their longest sides. Their width varies from 50 to 80 cm.

It is rare though that a dovecote is so small that the two-meter slabs cover the entire distance between the walls (usually the space to be covered is three meters). The problem is solved as follows: at one-meter height, sometimes less, the inner walls widen (a sort of corbelling) and eventually get close enough together that a slab two meters wide bridges them. Depending on the dovecote in question, only the inner walls of the two longest sides will so widen (drawing I) or, alternatively, all four walls can be so treated.

If the distance between the walls exceeds 3.5 m, and always if no wood-joists are involved, other solutions are required. One solution is to build an arch (drawing II), usually slightly curved. Often, the arch itself widens at its top, so as to further reduce the expanse for the plates to close. There exists another, quite original, solution: the construction against one of the long walls of the dovecote of one or two stone walls on which slabs are placed running parallel to the main wall. All that remains is to cover the reduced space between these slabs and the opposite wall with medium-sized slabs (drawing III). This method can be used on protruding anta walls.

Some recent structures are covered with slabs or thin slabs, placed on the joist-beams.

8. This dovecote near Tarambados (17) is one of the most beautiful in all of Tinos thanks to its harmonious proportions, its complex decoration, and the high quality of the whole construction (see drawings pp. 72–75).

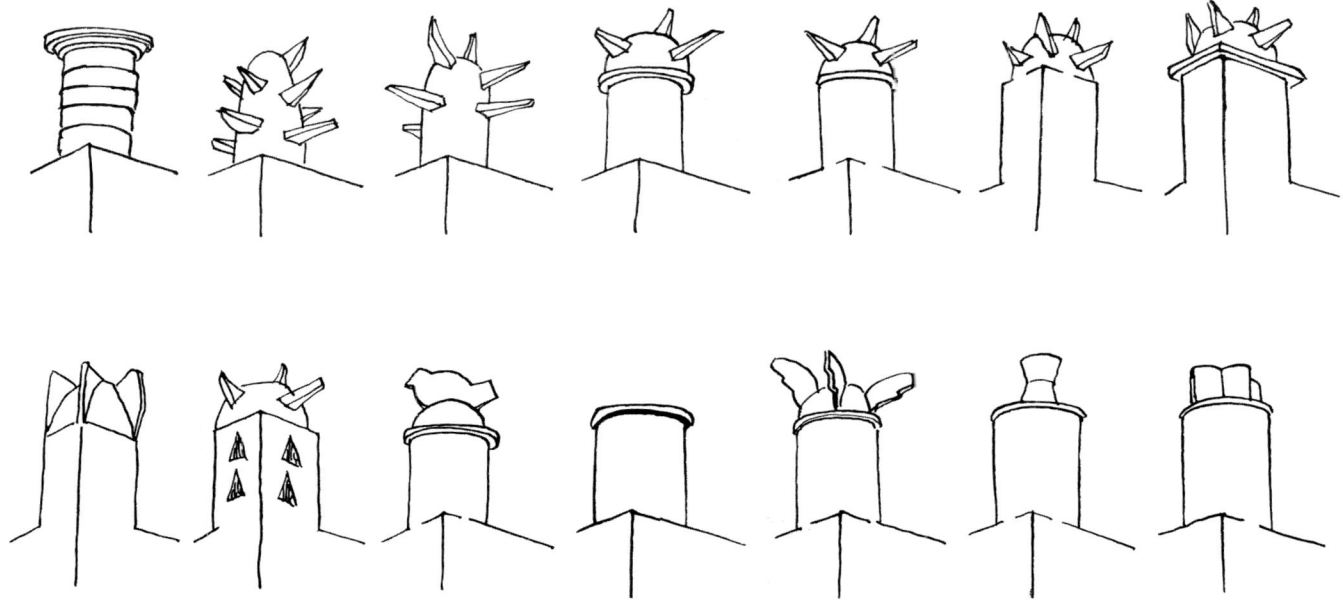

THE ELEMENTS OF THE CROWNING OF THE DOVECOTES

The roof is always edged by a low wall, like a parapet, varying in height, which extends the line of the outer walls and collects rainwater into a couple of gutters, placed on the interior face. This low wall can be up to a meter high, and is topped by a sometimes protruding slab or is rounded off. It is usually enlivened with small columns, banquettes and sharp paving slabs, (barbed slate).

9. This wonderful old dovecote is located near Tarambados (21). Unfortunately, it is collapsing, but still retains the high columns at its corners, and the banquette on the south facade (see drawings pp. 82–83).

The **columns** are small solid stone structures, of a square or circular shape, from 40 cm to 1 m high. They are always placed at the corners of the dovecotes, and exceptionally above a facade, replacing the banquettes. Small thin and pointed slate slabs ("needles"), intended primarily for perches for the pigeons, are embedded into the columns. The columns also have a decorative role, as they emphasize the corners of the dovecote. In Tinos, we find such columns only in dovecotes, never in domestic architecture. The crowning of the building can also consist mainly of slabs of stone (pillars), roughly shaped and irrespective of the columns, which they replace quite often, mainly in the area of the village of Pyrgos. In some cases, they are grotesquely shaped to frighten off predators: they are then called "cuckoos".

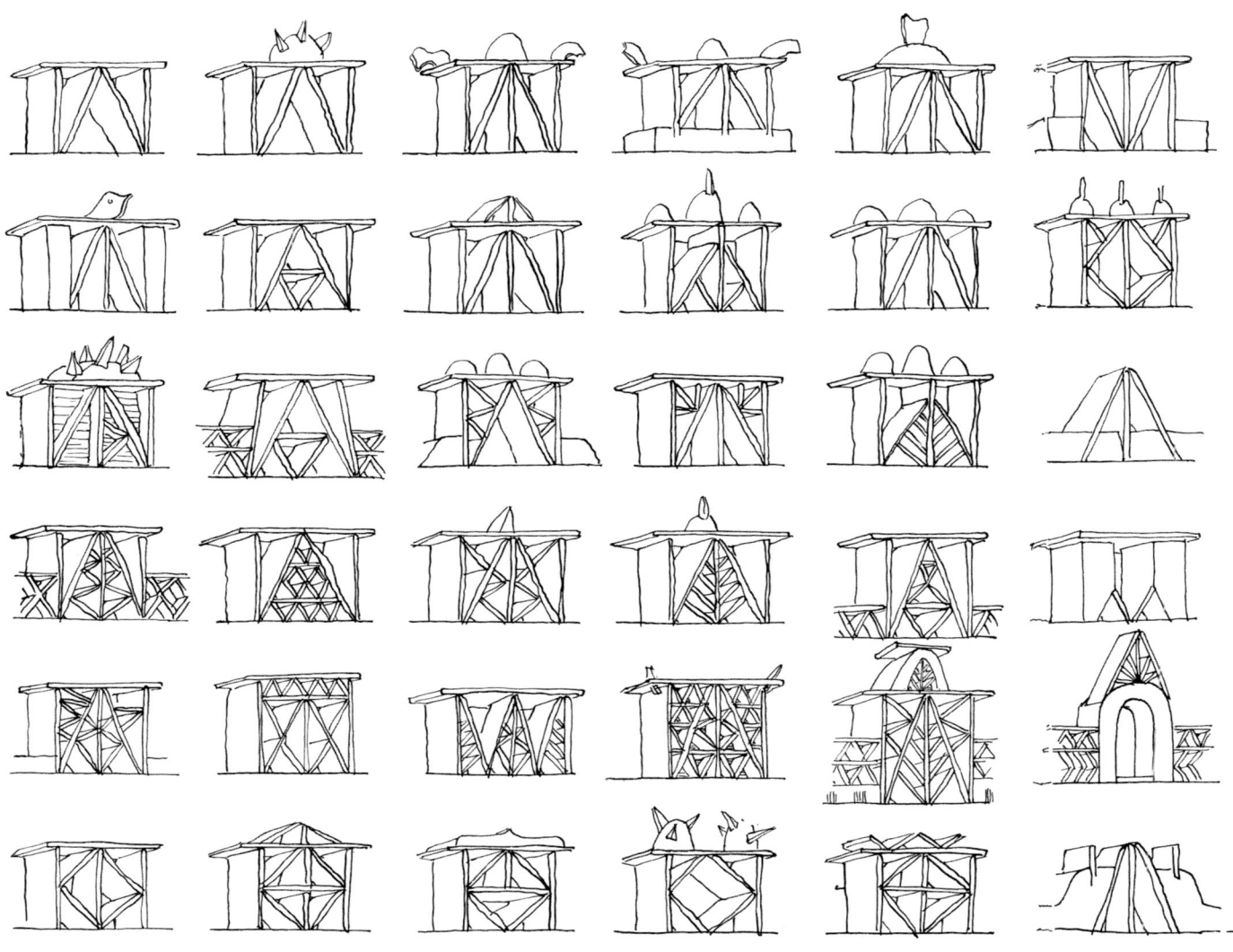

The **"banquettes"** are so named because, in their most basic form, they look like a bench, consisting of two vertical uprights and a small horizontal plank between. We see them on most dovecotes, above all the decorated facades or only above the main facade. Sometimes, many banquettes are found on the same facade in the case of the richly decorated dovecotes. They are also intended, like the columns, for perches.

They also contribute to the richness of the decoration, if we compare them with the dovecotes of Andros, which

usually do not have such a feature: their absence significantly impairs the appearance of the facades.
The two upright panels of a banquette are usually embedded into the capping wall or, more rarely, into the decorated wall. The horizontal slab sometimes carries one or many masonry plaques. On several dovecotes on the island, we can find numerous variations on the theme of the banquette but they always serve the same function.

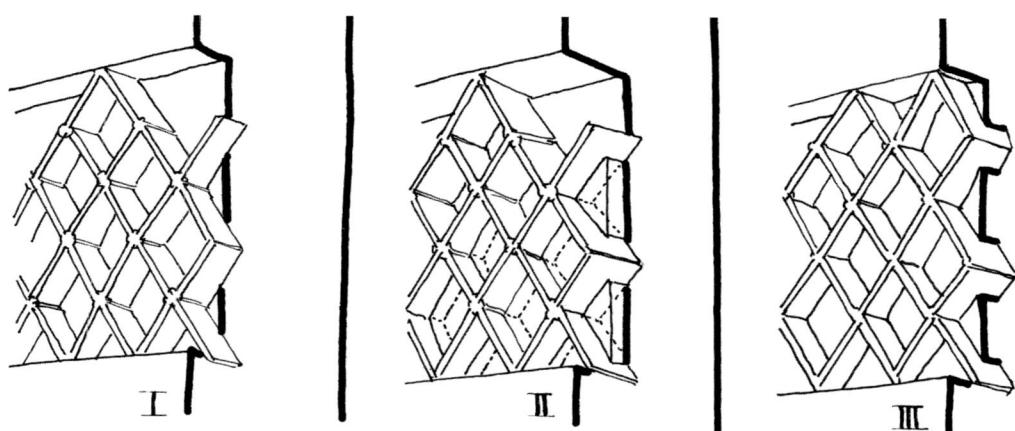

THE COMPOSITION OF THE DECORATION

The three basic decorative elements are the diamond-shaped rhombus, the sun and the cypress tree. The originality of the Tenian dovecote is due to their varied appearance and combinations. We will refer later to the origin, significance and transformations of these motifs. But first, let's see how they are composed: with slabs of stone, placed in the niches of the facade. The slabs are of schist, less often of marble. They are 2 to 4 cm thick, 8 to 12 cm wide and their length varies from 6 to 15 cm, sometimes more.

They are placed in various manners, as shown in the picture above. The fastest way to work is to place the slabs in the niche so that they rest on top of each other (Fig. I). It is a fragile construction, even if small plaster-mortar marbles are added to the points where the slabs are jointed together. For this reason, the niche is usually made a little deeper, in order that there be placed at the back, between the slabs, a fairly thick layer of mortar (Fig. II). Rarely is the decorative arrangement of slabs made at the same time as the wall is put up (Fig. III).

The rhombus motif (Figs. IV and V) is often combined with horizontal slabs, which facilitate the construction and increase the stability of the decoration.

The sun and cypress motif are made in a similar way, set in circular or triangular niches. Often, the cypress branches are wedged in place using the depth of the niche to hold them (Fig. VI). Otherwise, small stones must be added alongside the trunk (Fig. VII). The circular niche surrounding the sun is more difficult to construct (Figs. VIII to XIII). Usually, one or more sunrays are wedged in the masonry around the niche (Fig. XI – XIII).

Rhombi, suns and cypresses are the oldest and most common motifs. Very often they are used together in the same frieze, merging into each other. One can imagine the endless variety of combinations that can occur: I recorded over

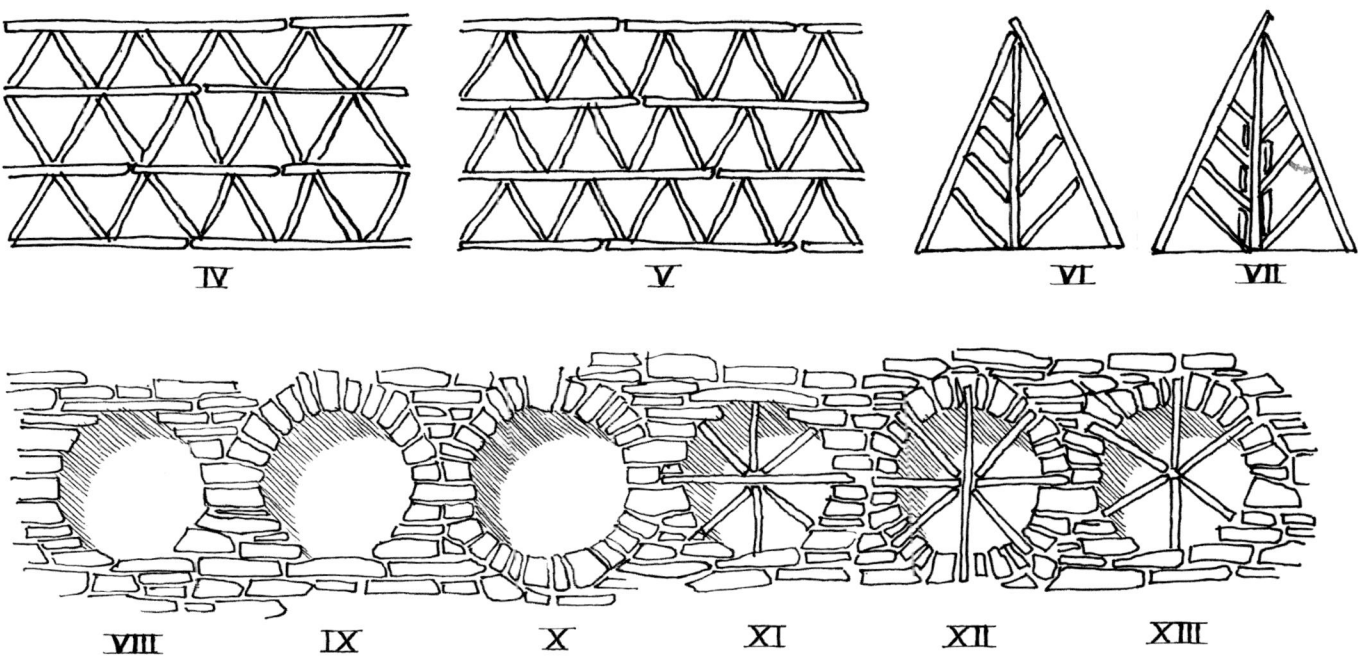

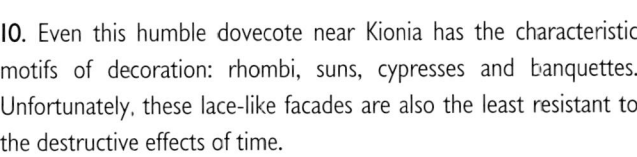

450! Only in the area of Kato Meri do other patterns appear: tiles and herringbones.

The decoration is sometimes left uncoated and sometimes plastered. For a better standard of construction, the facade and slabs need to be whitewashed, while the ground of the decoration remains uncoated. Then the design stands out well against the background, and as one villager told me: "When a pigeon sits on a nest, you see it from afar: a white dot on a black background."

10. Even this humble dovecote near Kionia has the characteristic motifs of decoration: rhombi, suns, cypresses and banquettes. Unfortunately, these lace-like facades are also the least resistant to the destructive effects of time.

THE ORIGIN OF THE DECORATIVE MOTIFS

But why did they choose suns, cypresses and rhombi? Do these patterns mean something? Why are they so prevalent? And, first of all, where do they come from?
Such motifs have existed in the East since antiquity, perhaps since prehistoric times. The solar disk and its derivative forms (rosettes, discs with curved rays, wheels, crosses, etc.) were symbols of the sun, a source of life. We find them in Egypt, Assyria, and on the funerary larnakes of the Macedonian royal dynasty. The same goes for the triangle, which symbolizes the wind and lightning, and is, like the circle, a perfect shape, a symbol of all trinities. As for the cypress, it was in the Ancient East, in Phoenicia and in Cyprus an important religious symbol: the tree of life, symbol of the god Mithras.
Later, these motifs lost their religious character, but retained a magical, protective value: at the beginning of the last century, the roofs of some Polish farmhouses were decorated with horns and with nails intended to ward off the devil. We can find similar examples everywhere.
These motifs have survived to this day in folk art. They have in turn lost both their religious and magical value, and are considered merely decorative elements. Sometimes, they even lose their basic identification: for a villager, the sun is nothing more than a simple windmill, while the cypress is a fishbone.

II. Excellently preserved and freshly whitewashed, this dovecote (31) is located near the beach, below the village of Kardiani (see drawings pp. 94, 95).

THE TRANSFORMATIONS OF THE CYPRESS TREE

The transformations the cypress underwent show how a decorative motif can be modified according to the needs imposed by the construction method. The cypress is a motif that is often used in Greek folk art, mainly on wooden or stone objects. In embroidery, floral patterns are usually preferred (but not always), as they are more flexible and richer. The presence of the cypress on dovecotes raises a question. Is it a reproduction of a folk-art motif in stone? Or just a composition whose sole purpose is to fill a triangular niche? A careful examination of the dovecotes in fact shows that the purpose is to transfer a folk motif to stone.

Indeed, the most common type I cypress motif is difficult to reproduce in a dovecote: the slabs that make up the branches are unstable. The sub-type I.1, mentioned above, demonstrates by its complexity the desire to transfer a traditional motif to the decoration of the dovecotes. Most of the other types of the cypress motif arose from the search to find an easier way of construction: in examples 1.2 and 1.3, all the oblique slabs converge at the base of the triangle, so that they are held in place by themselves. Similarly, the slabs of 1.4 and 1.6 are set parallel to the oblique sides of the rectangle. Types 1.7 to 1.11, set in a niche of other shapes, are quite common in the Kato Meri and in the upper part of the valley of Kome. The pot in which the cypress of 1.8 is planted is also found in the embroidery: it is further proof that the decorative motifs of the dovecotes are really drawn from the old anthology of folk art.

The type II cypress is not much removed from the type I: one of the two branches is placed slanted in the opposite direction, so the slabs support each other. Sub-types IV.1 and IV.2 combine elements of I and II. Examples of Type III are much rarer, and they no longer really draw their inspiration from the cypress. The cypresses of types V and VI fit somewhere between the previous ones. Only once did I notice a cypress of type VII.

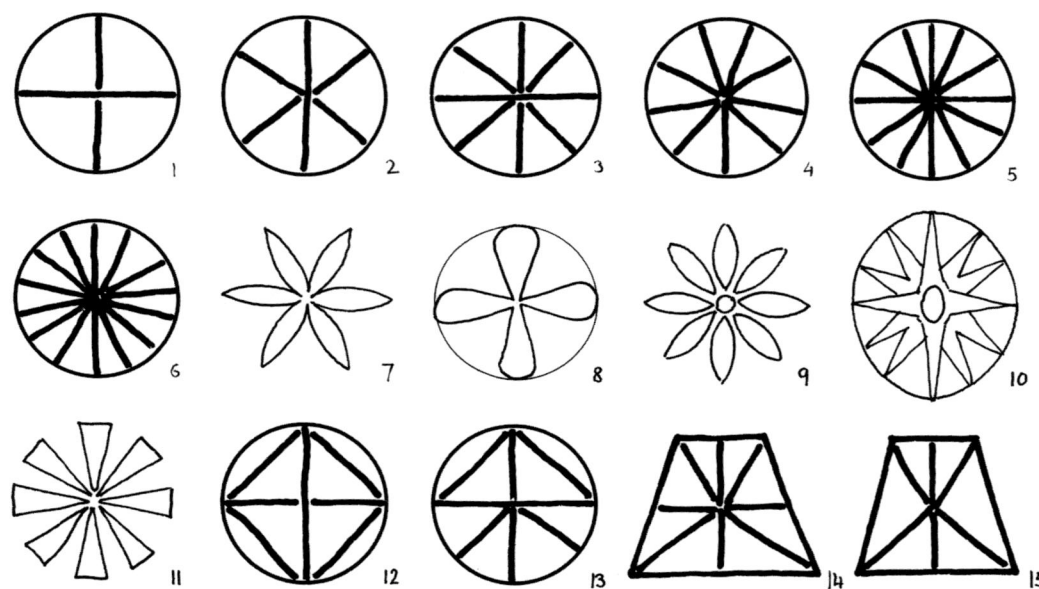

THE VARIATIONS ON THE SUN MOTIF

The sun is also a fundamental feature of folk art: it has a limited number of basic types, with almost infinite variations. Types 1–6, set in the niches, are the most common. They differ from each other in the number of rays.
More rarely, we encounter different types:
7. A rosette painted on the facade of dovecotes in the area of Pyrgos.
8. A low relief version, on a stone disk.

9 and 11. Suns drawn in a hollow of the facade of dovecotes in Kato Meri.
10. Suns carved onto a marble slab: the rays stand out against the dark background of the stonework.
12 and 13. Suns which are again set in niches, sometimes circular and sometimes polygonal (14 & 15).

12. The impressive dovecote 18, built in two successive phases with but a small time difference, is also located near Tarambados (see drawings pp. 76–77).

FROM THE LIMITATIONS OF FOLK ARCHITECTURE …

The dovecotes of Tinos are a perfect example of the role played by some inescapable limitations affecting folk architecture. Equipped with limited technical means, the craftsman cannot escape the local conditions, it being impossible to modify a material for some use for which it is not intended. The dovecote of Tinos would not have been adorned with its lace-like slabs, if the rocks of the island did not consist of layers of slate, a *sine qua non*.

The craftsman also has to comply with practical scopes. He must, first of all, deliver a functional building that meets strictly defined needs. Aesthetic criteria can never get in the way. Rather a decorative element might result from a necessity. The crook of the Greek shepherd is the perfect example. Similarly, the decoration of the dovecotes provides the birds with perches protected from the winds.

The submission of the craftsman to strict rules explains the universality of folk art. Similar creations appear in areas very distant from each other. In some farmhouses in the Vendée region (France), for example, the decorative arrangement pictured below, made by placing stones on top of each other, is known. They fashioned these "baptismal bouquets" to celebrate the completion of a farmhouse, as elsewhere they plant a fir tree decorated with ribbons. The similarity between these "bouquets" and the banquettes of the dovecotes of Tinos is impressive. It is explained if we take into account that the materials used are similar, as well as by the fact that decorative vocabulary is both limited in form and often common. The same feeling that prevails in the construction of these French "bouquets" might as well exist in Tinos.

We will see on the following pages that the conception of the decoration may vary, ranging from classical self-restraint to excessive extravagance. The facade of some dovecotes is covered with intertwined decorative patterns. Other examples have simpler facades, decorated in moderation. In all cases, however, the decoration is limited to the facades that welcomed the pigeons' arrival, while large areas remain undecorated.

However, the sense of moderation does not stop here. I was impressed that in Tinos the elaborate decoration of the dovecotes is never applied in houses. A villager gave me an explanation: "A house is a whole, with rooms, with doors and windows, with people and animals. It is something alive, it does not need decoration. On the other hand, a dovecote would be very ugly without decoration: a simple, square building with holes and nothing else. It would be something lifeless."

13. Fishermen pull their nets, somewhere between Kionia and Agios Romanos. Such images have tended to disappear: the development of tourism comes at a price.

... TO THE CREATION OF A STYLE

From all these restraints there nonetheless emerged a manner of construction that we do not find anywhere else, a style with its own rules, its characteristic forms, its traditions. A very flexible style, one which can always be adapted to the very different conditions affecting the construction of a dovecote, while at the same time it is in itself very strict and unchanging: to make the point, it is enough to recall how many of the dovecotes made today look like those of the 18th century.

Nevertheless, modifications do occur with the introduction of new forms and new decorative motifs: there are examples in Kato Meri, dating from the late 19th century, and similar attempts were being made when I was visiting the Pyrgos area. These attempts are usually doomed, failing to become an integral part of the style. Sometimes, though — as in the case of the introduction of the banquette — a craftsman manages to create a form that becomes part of the tradition and is adopted as a characteristic element of the style.

We will now make some tours around Tinos, to present its most beautiful dovecotes, but also to experience representative examples of the various "schools". We will also present some of the most humble dovecotes, which nonetheless have interesting constructions.

13

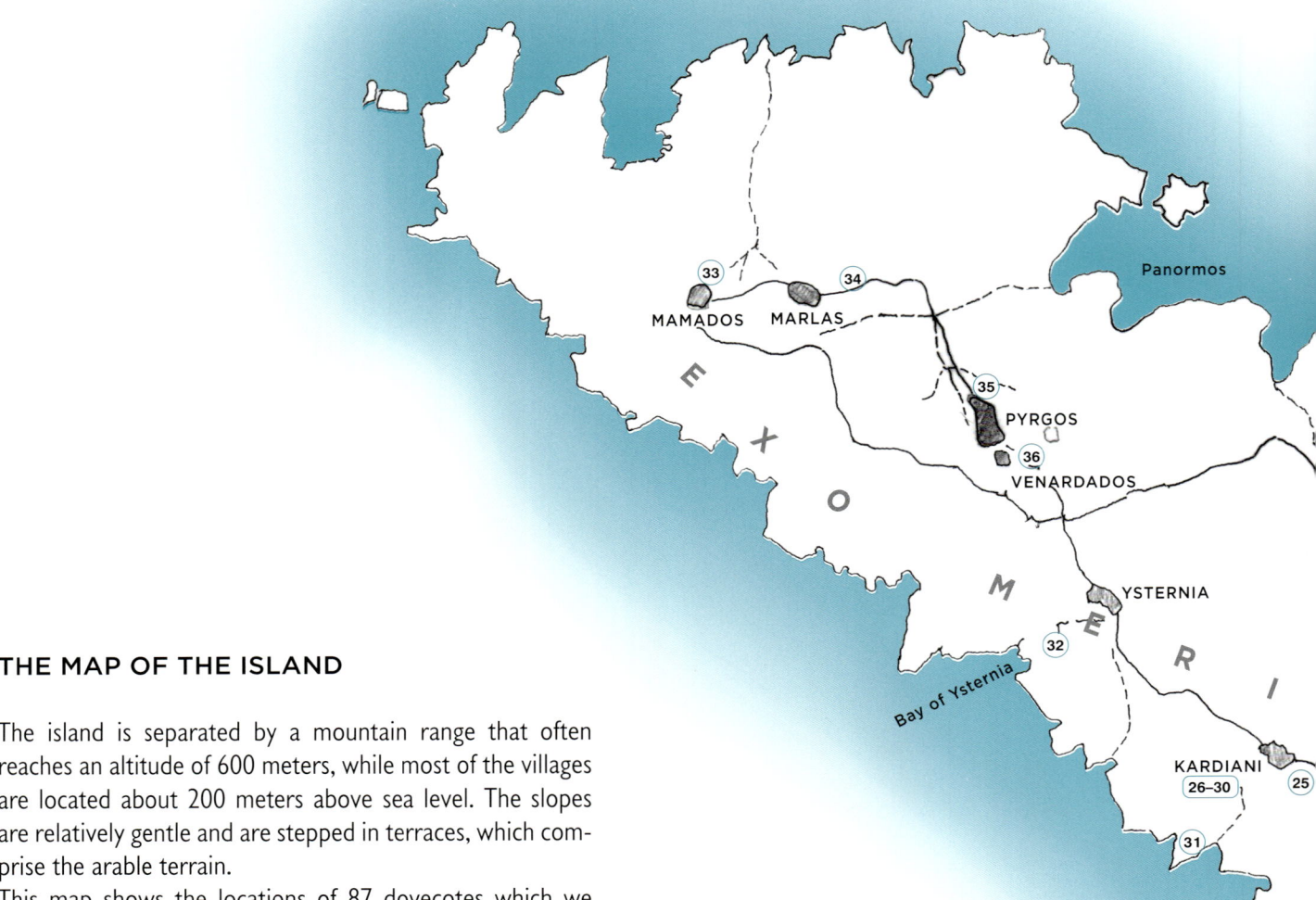

THE MAP OF THE ISLAND

The island is separated by a mountain range that often reaches an altitude of 600 meters, while most of the villages are located about 200 meters above sea level. The slopes are relatively gentle and are stepped in terraces, which comprise the arable terrain.

This map shows the locations of 87 dovecotes which we describe in the following pages. We divided them into three zones, which are recommended here for the visitor:

Route 1 (Dovecotes 1–32): The west coast of the island, from the bay of Kionia, west of the port, to Ysternia. Next comes the zone of marble bedrock, which reaches up to the north-western tip of the island, not far from the neighbouring island of Andros.

Route 2 (Dovecotes 33–60): The north coast of Tinos, with its two inhabited areas: that of Pyrgos and then of Komi, with its many small valleys.

Route 3 (Dovecotes 61–87): The southeast coast. Below Exomvourgo, at 641 m, is the plateau of Steni, and many valleys that run down to the sea.

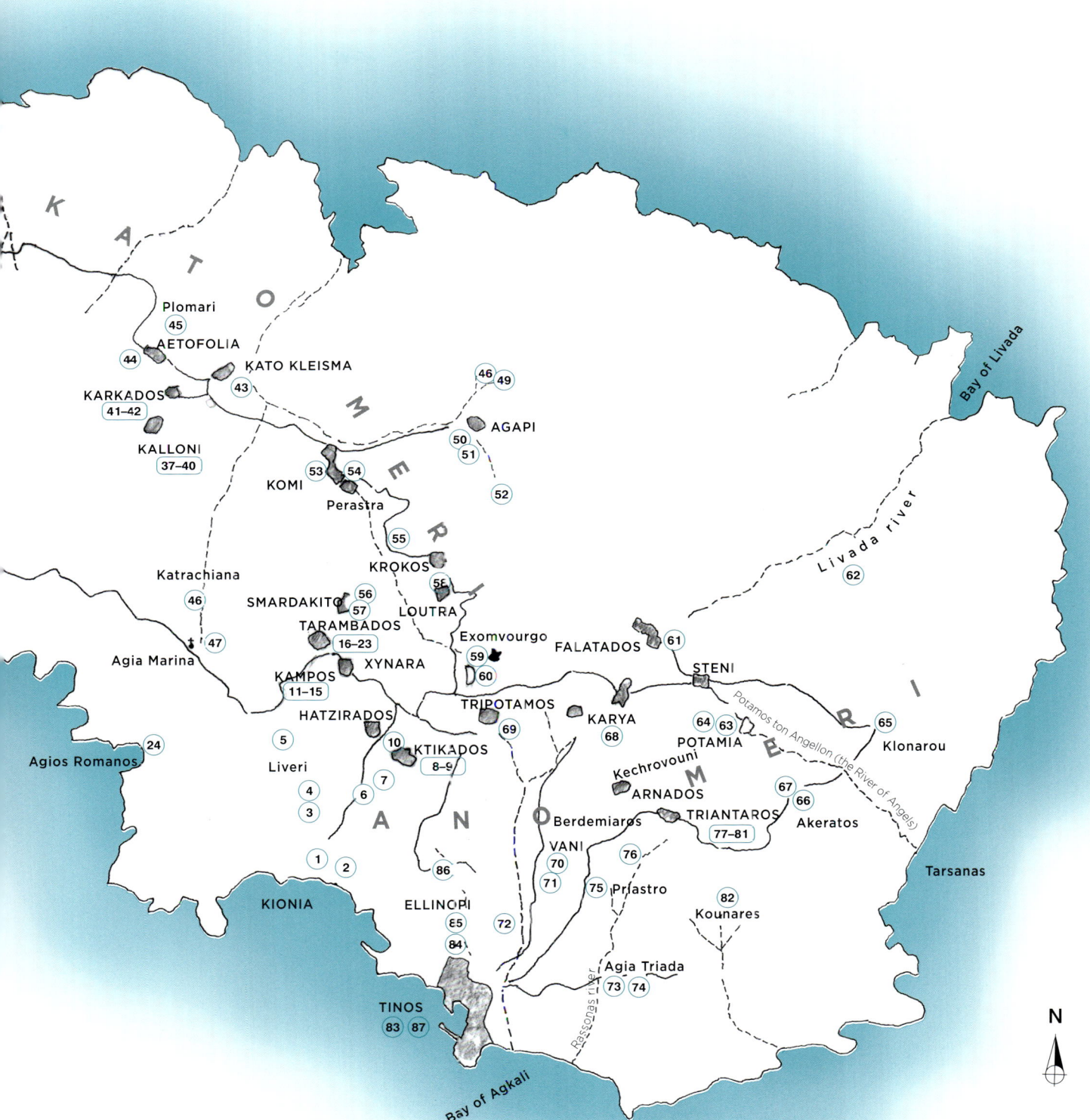

FIRST ROUTE

WEST COAST: FROM KIONIA TO KTIKADOS, HATZIRADOS, TARAMBADOS AND KARDIANI

Facing southwest, the indented coastline unfolds in small picturesque coves from the port of Tinos (Chora) to the cape located opposite Andros. It is a fertile area with many springs and wells, rich in crops and vegetables, as well as many olive trees. From the bay in Kionia, we ascend to the beautiful villages of Ktikados and Hatzirados, admiring the stepped terraces that manifest the effects of human effort on the landscape. From up above, we have an unobstructed view of the village of Tarambados, surrounded by its wonderful traditional dovecotes. We continue on to Kardiani, with its glittering white houses and its dovecotes that run down to the sea. Further on, the route continues to the historical village of Ysternia, birthplace of great sculptors such as the Fitali and Malakate brothers, the Sochoi, Georgios Vitalis and the younger Lazaros Lameras. Even further north, begins the area of large marble quarries, where there are no water sources and therefore no dovecotes.

14. A stepped cobbled path (*kalderimi*) to the south of Tarambados, leading to some of the most beautiful dovecotes on the island.

15. The valley that descends to Kionia is rich in trees, crops and meadows.

16. Like dovecote 1 photographed by Fred Boissonas (see Fig. 1), this dovecote (4) is located in the valley that ends at the beach in Kionia (see drawing p. 54).

17. Dovecote 2 has its ground floor acting as a temporary storage space for tools or agricultural products. It is located in the small valley of Liveri, above Kionia (see drawings pp. 50–51).

18. Dovecote 18 near Tarambados (see also p. 35, as well as drawings pp. 76–77).

19. Dovecote 17 is close to the previous ones, and is one of the most beautiful on the island (see also p. 23, as well as drawings pp. 72–75).

20. At the entrance of Tarabamdos is dovecote 16, one of the very rare examples on the island, where the dovecote is attached to the wall of a house (see drawings pp. 70–71).

21. View of the valley of Kardiani which has considerable amounts of vegetation and crops on terraces. There are scattered dovecotes right down to the beach.

22–23. Two images from the interior of dovecote 27 in the valley of Kardiani (see description and drawing p. 90).

1 KIONIA

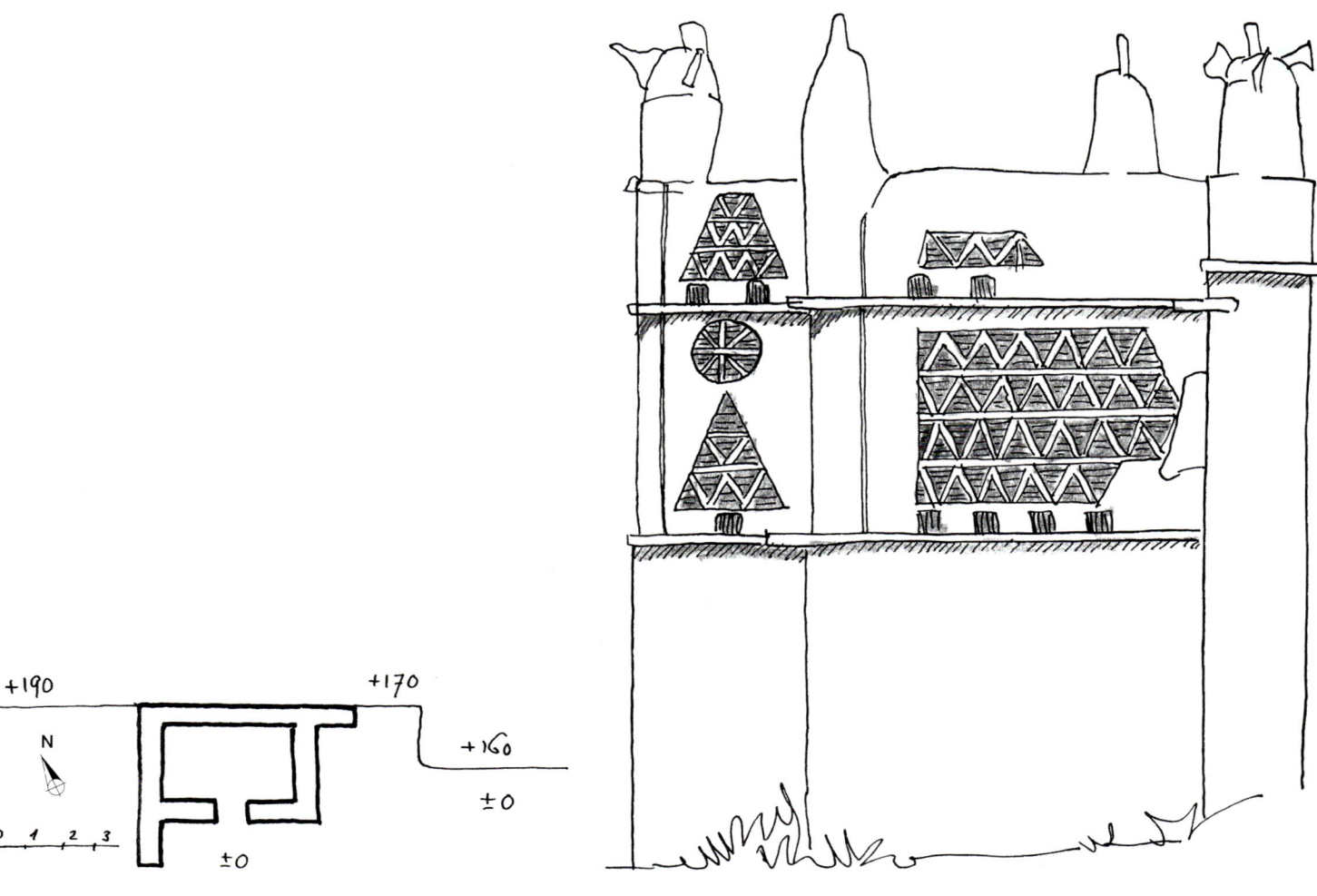

East facade

KIONIA, west of the city of Tinos, is a large bay, where between two rocky capes, stretches one of the most beautiful beaches on the island. The villagers go down there to cultivate their fields. Small windmills are found there and a draw-well, driven by a donkey walking in a circle and with its eyes blindfolded, hauls up water from an underground aquifer. Some fishermen live there in the summer.

One of them, E. Lefkaros, owns a dovecote still occupied by pigeons (1). Until 1922, it was a beautiful edifice, with the upper frieze decorated with three cypress trees and above it a row of smaller cypress trees that alternated with suns. It was also photographed by Fred Boissonnas (p. 9). In the meantime, however, the roof has collapsed and two awkward restorations have left it in the current condition…

South facade

2 KIONIA

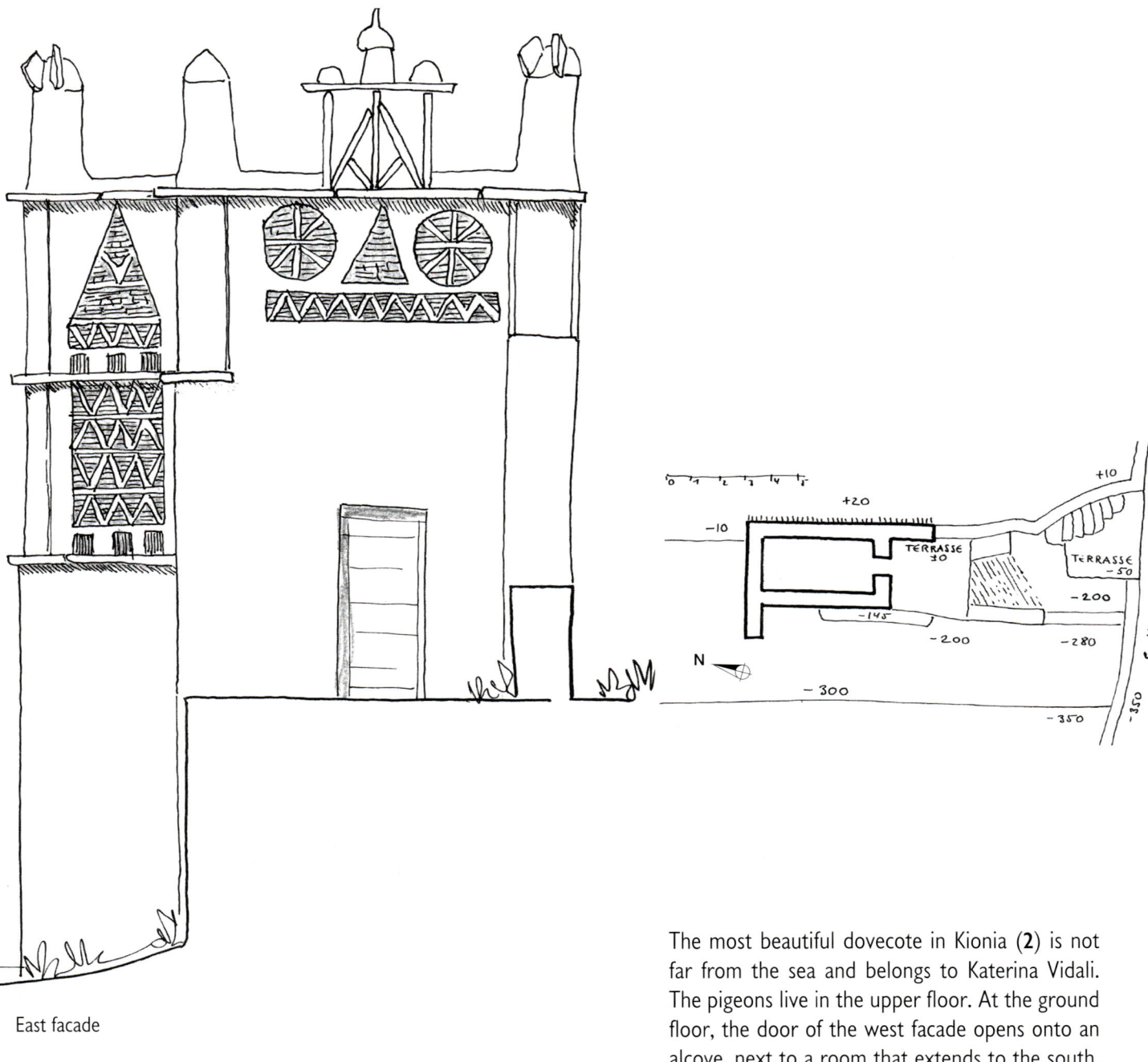

East facade

The most beautiful dovecote in Kionia (**2**) is not far from the sea and belongs to Katerina Vidali. The pigeons live in the upper floor. At the ground floor, the door of the west facade opens onto an alcove, next to a room that extends to the south, beyond the dovecote (see Fig. 17, p. 43).

South facade

3 KIONIA (LIVERI)

South-east facade

In Kionia, west of the beach, the small valley of **LIVERI** ascends to the chapel of Agia Marina. Here we find a dovecote (**3**), with interesting carved slabs on the cornice of the anta walls. It belongs to a certain Foskolos from Hatzirados, and is located in the centre of a land plot. It is accompanied by a threshing floor, where they thresh the wheat, and then winnow it at night, under a golden moonlight.

South-west facade

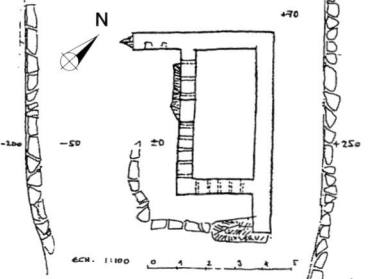

4 KIONIA (LIVERI)

South facade

East facade

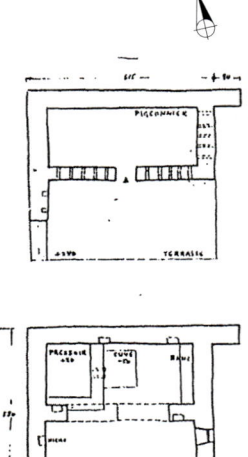

Higher in the small valley, we see an abandoned dovecote (**4**), which belongs to Antonios Foskolos. The ground floor consists of a large room with fireplace, bench and wine press. It is divided by a large arch, on which rests the wall of the storey where the pigeons once lived. The slabs are placed on roughly squared beams, which support a layer of clayey soil.

The rare in the area rounded corners and circular slabs, which are placed in the background of the sun motifs, as well as an exceptional affinity in style with dovecote 6, make us assume that the two dovecotes could be works of the same craftsman (see Fig. 16, p. 43).

Even higher up, a large dovecote (**5**), in a nice, well-irrigated garden, dominates the small barren valley of Liveri. Old but well plastered, it belongs to a resident of Kampos. It differs in style from the previous ones: it has rounded corners and rows of rectangles decorated with rhombi. The semicircular arches above them have the appearance of niches. It carries a rich, detailed decoration, reminiscent of that of the dovecotes of Smardakito.

KIONIA (LIVERI) 5

6 FROM KIONIA TO KTIKADOS

A paved path ascends from Kionia to **KTIKADOS**. It passes in front of the dovecote (**6**) of Frangiskos Tassiras, built 120 years ago by his great-grandfather, and still in excellent condition. The two decorated facades are plastered and whitewashed, while the others were not plastered, for reasons of economy. The same decoration continues on the east facade.

This dovecote has many peculiarities: reduction of the thickness of the walls in successive refurbishments, small square columns that have replaced the corner posts, and stonework behind the banquette.

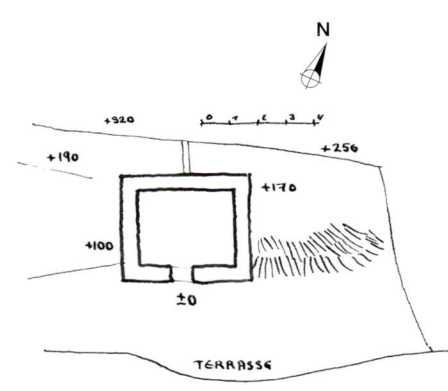

KTIKADOS 7

The village of **KTIKADOS** forms a long crescent of white houses. A large olive grove descends from the village. Some orange trees, a more vivid note among the duller olive trees, and the few cypresses that rise up in the sky, complete the beautiful landscape.

At the entrance of the village is the dovecote of Giannis Vizinezos (**7**), which was built about fifty years ago. The southeast facade has decorated friezes and small openings. The banquette of the south-east facade consists of a tall carved stone, while that of the northeast facade consists of a tall vertically-set slate slab.

8 BETWEEN KIONIA AND KTIKADOS

In the olive groves, between Kionia and **KTIKADOS**, the most beautiful dovecote of the area is now sadly abandoned: since 1955 the roof had collapsed, destroying its interior (**8**).

A large ground floor room with an arch running through it and covered with slate at the tops of the walls and the arch, served as an animal shelter. A vertical staircase led from there to the roof (at a height of 3.60 above the ground level), in front of the entrance of the main dovecote.

The decoration of the exterior walls is a wonderful example of the typical style of the area: alternating suns and cypresses, and columns with strangely carved slabs. One of the ground floor walls rests, three meters below, on a terraced roof. There was still then a small cellar.

South-west facade

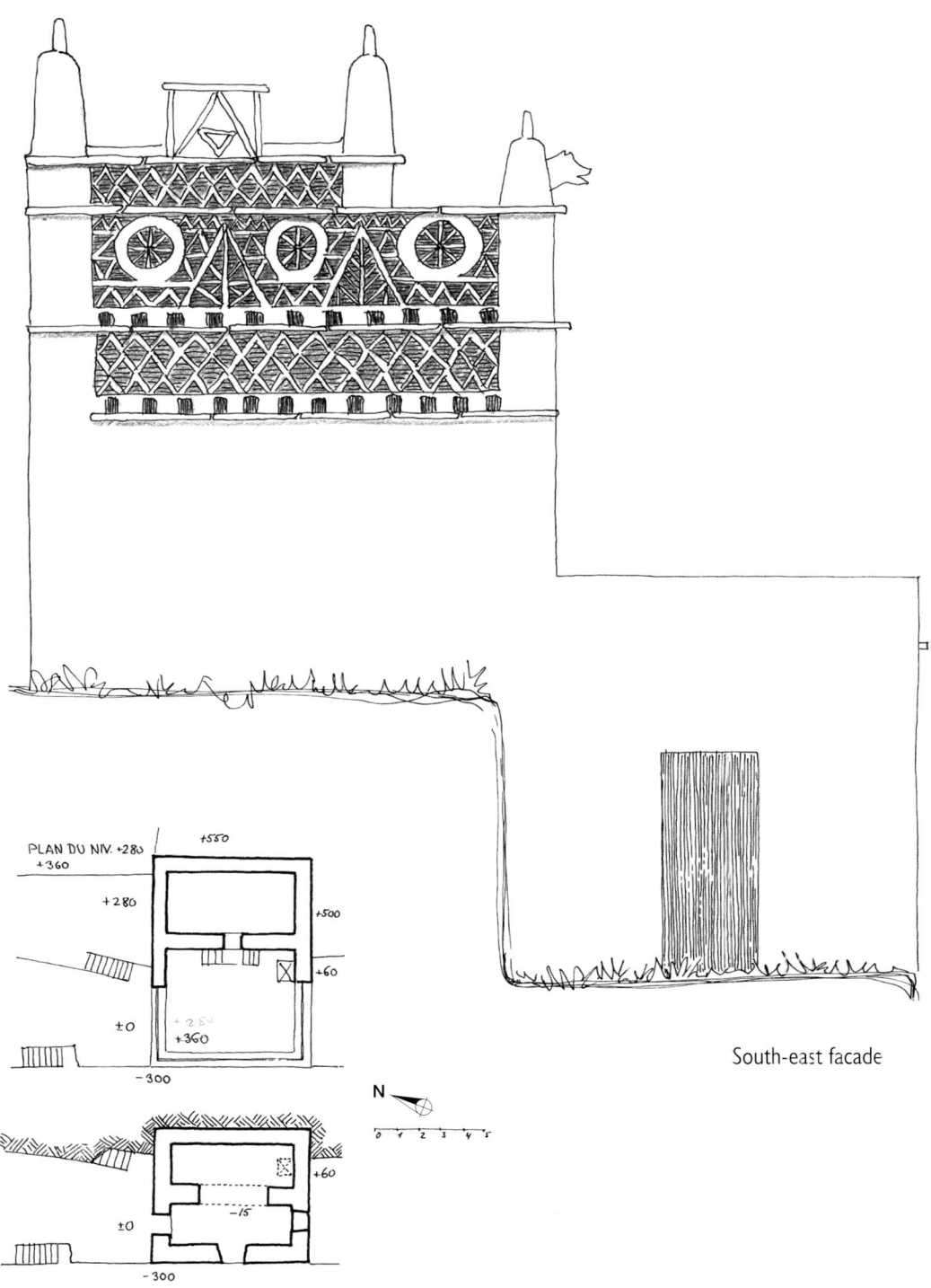

South-east facade

9 BETWEEN KIONIA AND HATZIRADOS

South-east facade

A paved path leads from **KTIKADOS** to **HATZIRADOS**. It passes by a mill, descends to a vaulted passage and ends at a fountain, between the two villages.

A very nice, whitewashed dovecote (**9**), which is about twenty years old, can be found there. It belongs to the teacher Antonios Siotos, and its decoration looks like light lace-work. The decorated sections are only a few centimetres deep: a dove could hardly find room to perch there. Blue plates —Chinese porcelains, with their traditional bridge, tree, and pagoda— are embedded in the wall. This arrangement is unique among the dovecotes of Tinos.

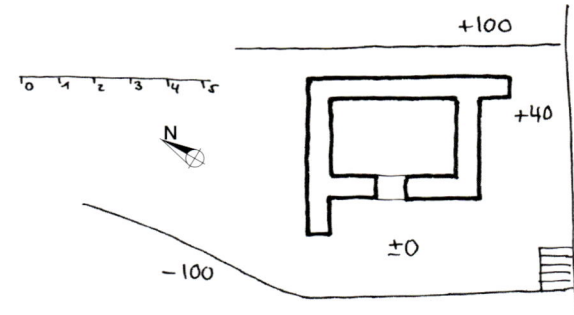

South-west facade

10 HATZIRADOS

A little further on, below **HATZIRADOS**, an old, ruined dovecote belongs to Filippos Samothrakis (**10**). The roof, made of slabs resting on beams, has collapsed.

It is a fairly old dovecote, with some rare features. Two long slate "needles" are inserted into the banquette. Small square pillars replace the columns. The only openings that allow access are under protruding slabs, a layout that is not well suited for the pigeons. Other openings are scattered about amongst the decorative rhombi.

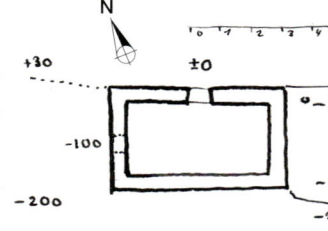

KAMPOS 11

Above **KAMPOS**, an uphill path starting from the road reaches a small spring and a garden with a dovecote (11), owned by Mathaios Filippousis. The ground floor is divided into two: a room, which serves to store tools, occupies the front of the building, while a hatchway allows the pigeons to descend from the main dovecote. We meet again those strange cypresses, set into semicircular niches. The anta wall extending the north facade was added at a later time than the construction of the dovecote proper.

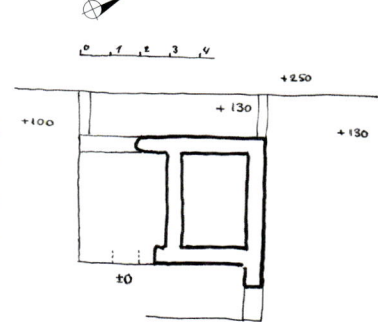

12 KAMPOS

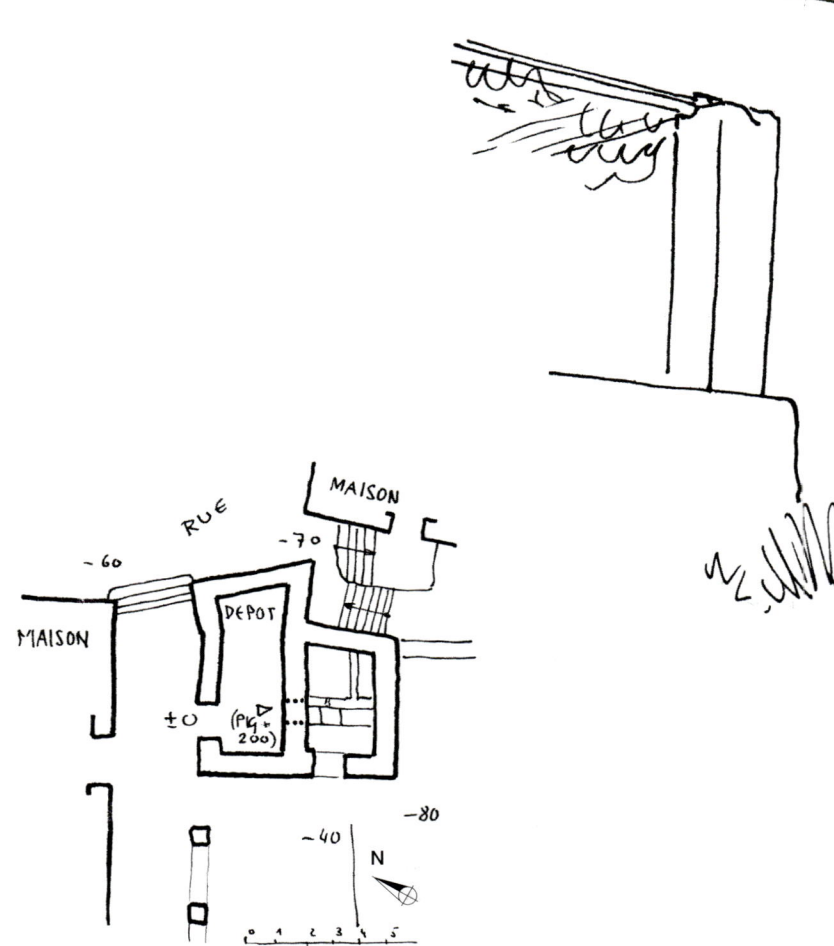

Inside the village, a beautiful dovecote goes with the house of Antonios Apergis (**12**). It is old, plastered and bright white. We may observe the decorative effect of the rounded corner, between the two facades.
Below the dovecote there is a wine-press: a large tank where grapes are pressed, with an opening from which they collect the grape juice, and a small tank where the must is stored before it is distilled. The entrance of the dovecote is by a small door that leads to the storeroom, at a height of two meters above ground level.

13 MESSARIA

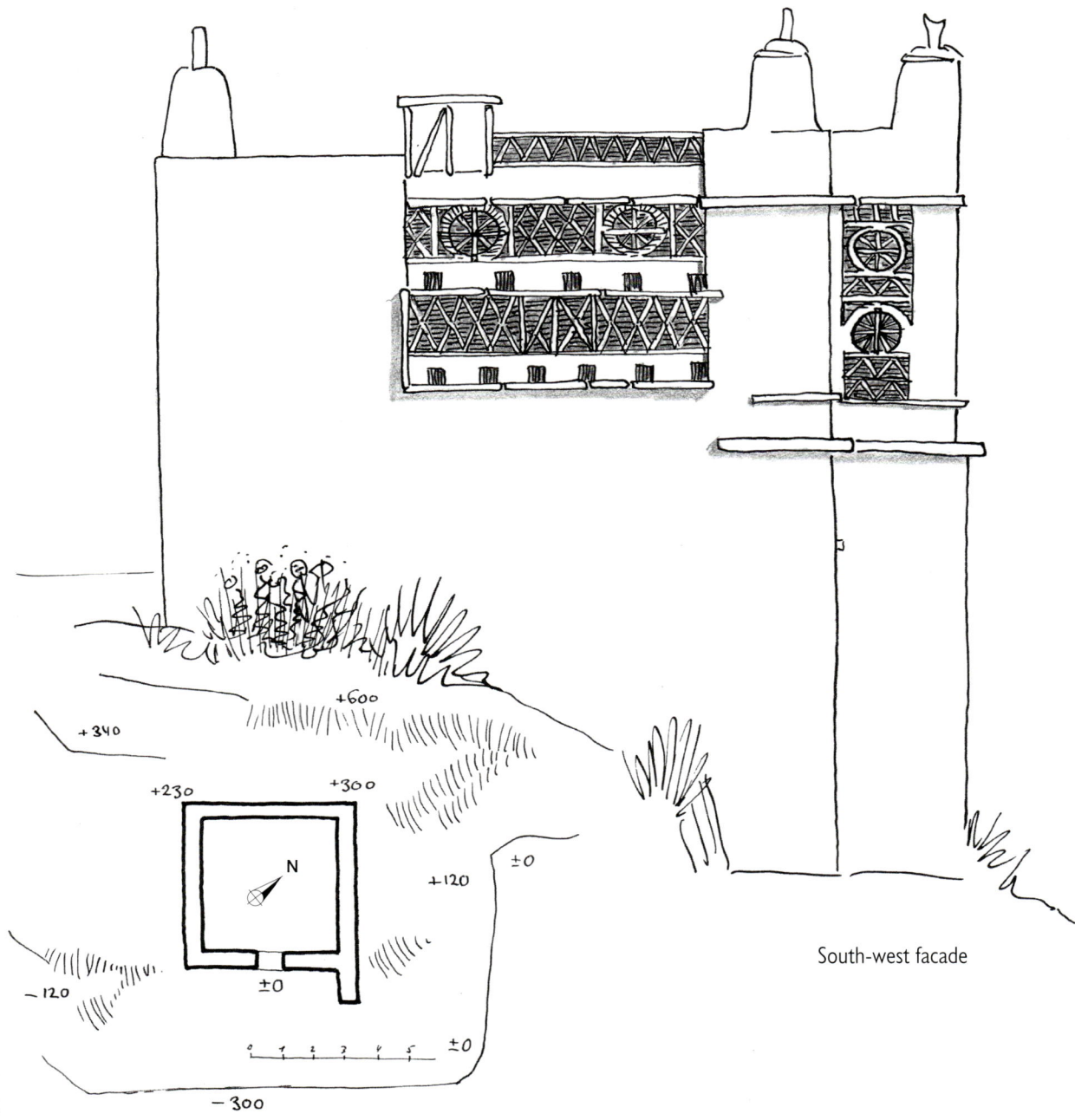

South-west facade

South-east facade

Just below the village of Kampos, a nice old dovecote (**13**) dominates a steep slope above Messaria. It belongs to a resident of the nearby village of Loutra, Nikolaos Provatinos. Its facade is very different from those of the previous dovecotes, as a pillar divides it in two: we encounter here again the influence of the dovecotes of Kato Meri, which we will look at later, and which is felt at Loutra. A nice old carved marble slab is placed above the door, with a beautiful decoration of cypresses and olives, boats (caravels) and flowers in vases.

14 KAMPOS

To the west of the village, a series of dovecotes, which all belong to the inhabitants of **KAMPOS**, succeed one another. One of them (**14**) belongs to Petros Kolaros. It is small and old, its two decorated facades (east and south) are plastered, while the other two are left uncoated. We may notice the anta wall, rounded and fully decorated, which is a rare occurrence, as well as an open-air staircase made of slabs, leading to the terraced roof. However, the first step of this is set quite high above the ground and it requires the help of a portable ladder to access it. The suns have been replaced by marble discs, each given four embossed carved petals. The same decoration continues on the east facade.

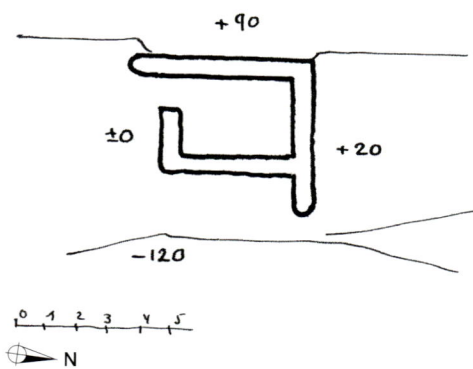

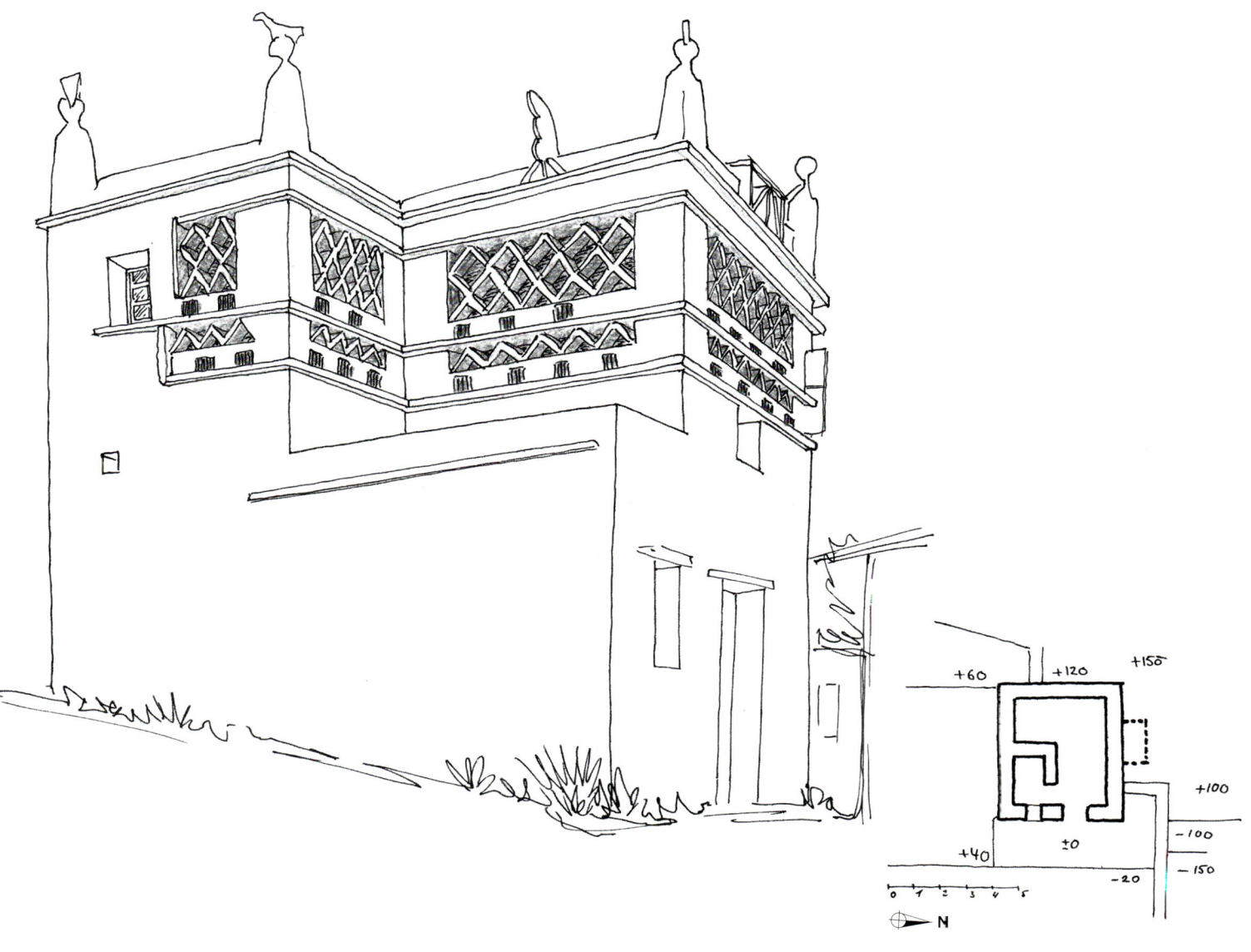

A little higher, an old, plastered dovecote (15), in a garden near a spring, belongs to Francisco Delatolas. The ground floor consists of a larger and a smaller room. To reinforce the north facade, which was in danger of collapsing, a stone wall has been added for support.

The first floor, where the pigeons live, is L-shaped, and is decorated only with rhombi. We may observe the columns: they are fashioned to resemble peacocks.

16 TARAMBADOS

South-west facade

Arriving in **TARAMBADOS** from the road that serves the western part of the island, we see a dovecote (**16**) situated in the corner of a house. This positioning is an extremely rare occurrence (see Fig. 20, p. 46). It has a rare type of cypress, as well as two rows of small openings, one above the other. Large carved marble slabs are placed above the doors and windows of the house. Above the entrance, one has an inscription in Latin:
THIS HOUSE WAS BUILT
BY IOANNIS KOUKOULAS (?), PRIEST
IN THE YEAR OF OUR LORD 1745

It is the oldest dated example of a dovecote I have come across, as it was obviously built together with the house. Two small, low-ceilinged rooms occupy the ground floor; we actually enter the dovecote from the roof of the house.

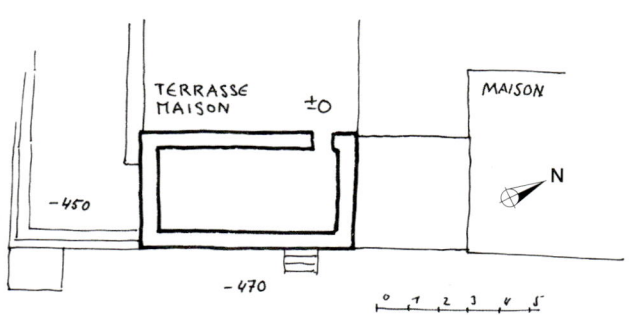

South-east facade

17 BELOW TARAMBADOS

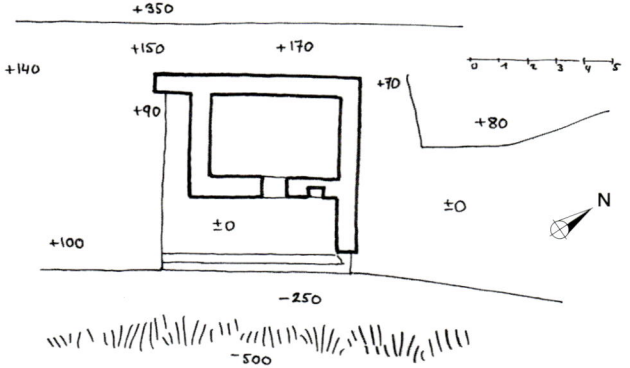

Below the village rises the most beautiful dovecote of the area, perhaps of the island. To reach it, one must descend to the small church located below the last houses of the village, where a path begins to run along the valley. Passing above fertile gardens, the path leads to a water-cistern, and then, under huge fig trees, to the water-source of the village, in the bed of the ravine (see Fig. p. 40). This dovecote (**17**) too is very old (probably dating to the 18th century). It owes its beauty to its balanced proportions, as it has been constructed with care and precision. It is adorned with three decorative friezes. The upper frieze, set on the wall surrounding the roof, is unusually tall. It has rhombi, but without small openings. A new decorative pattern makes its appearance here: tall rhombi ornamented with herringbone-shaped designs, in opposing pairs.

The south and northeast corners are rounded and covered with a light pink coating. Small columns, some of which are made of small cylindrical drums set one on top of another, rise at the corners of the dovecote and at the edges of the anta wall. Above there are monolithic capitals. The centre of the large facade is accentuated by an additional column framed by two banquettes with a stone backing, covered with slabs, into which thin slate "needles" are embedded (see Figs. 8 and 19, pp. 23 and 45).

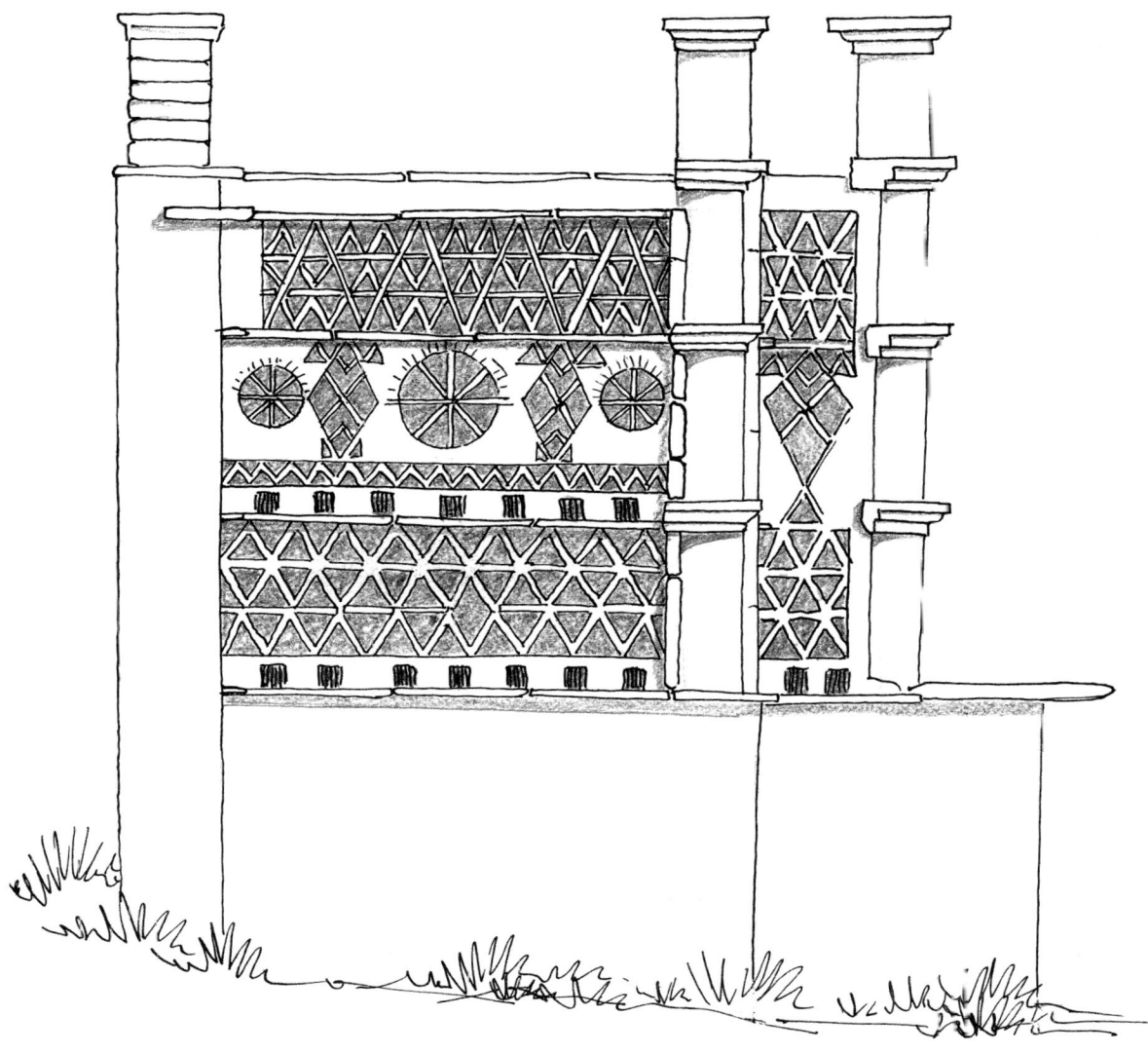

South-west facade

17 BELOW TARAMBADOS

North-west facade

South-east facade

18 BELOW TARAMBADOS

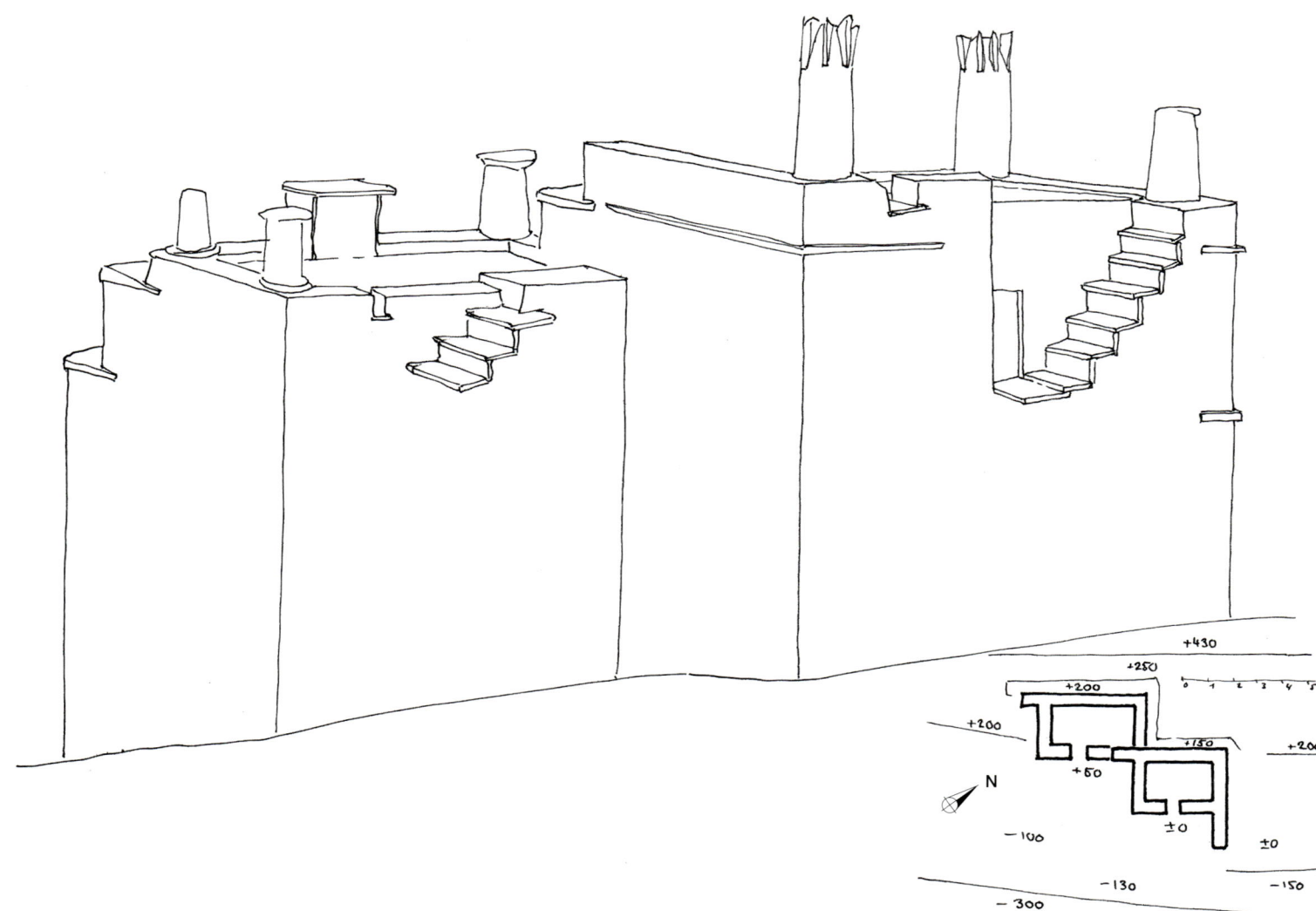

A little further down, on the left bank of the stream, above the irrigated fields, a dozen dovecotes are strung out in a row.

The first (**18**) we meet consists of two adjoining dovecotes. The oldest, to the east, that was built a long time ago, is decorated with small cypress trees at its corners. A little later, a second dovecote was built attached to the first: it is L-shaped, in order to be protected from the north wind. The anta wall of the old dovecote is incorporated as part of the facade of the newer one.

At some point, but still a long time ago, the upper part of the facade of the newest dovecote was destroyed, but was rebuilt with an anta wall that rests on the older one (see Fig. 12, p. 35).

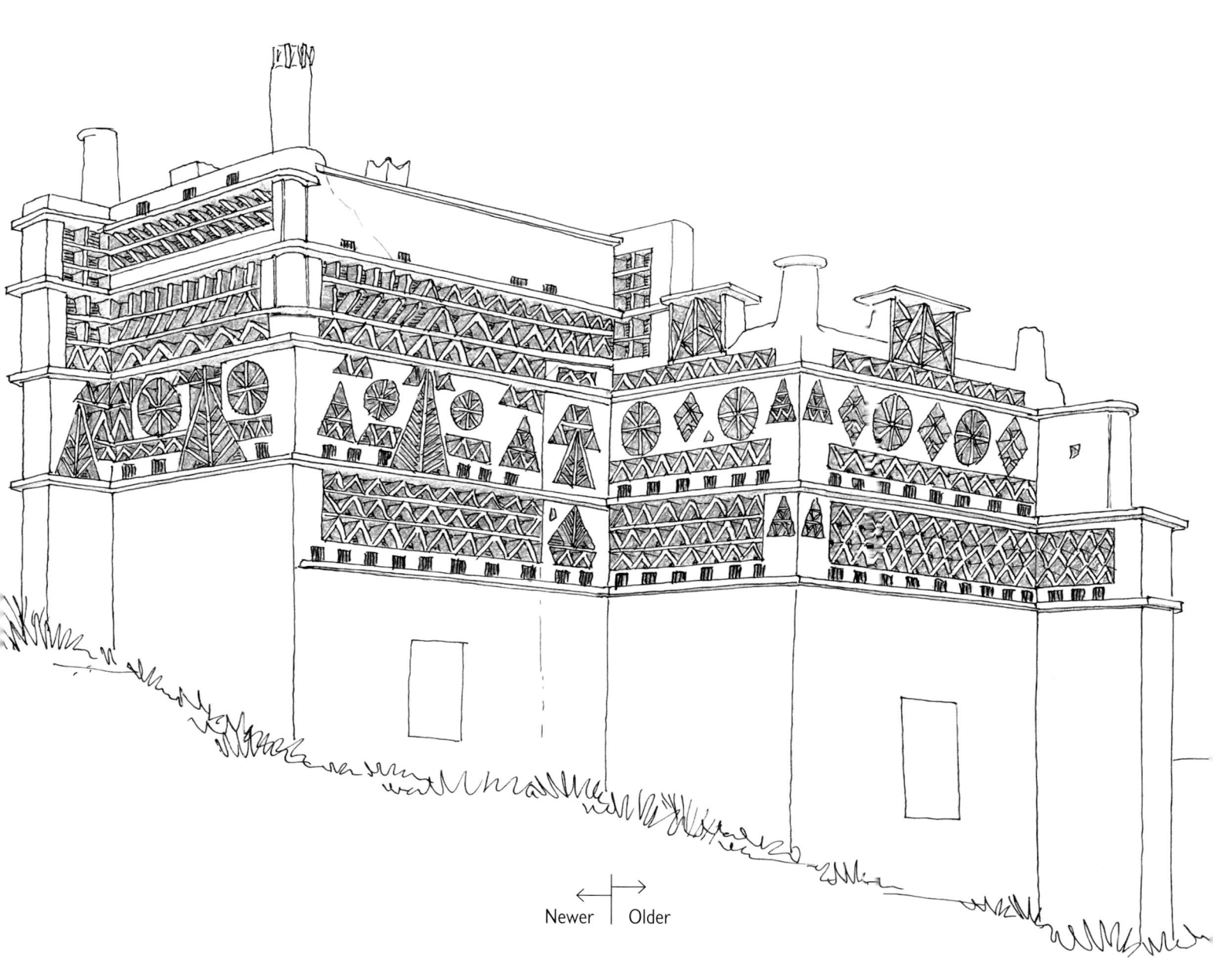

Newer | Older

19 TARAMBADOS

Another dovecote, belonging to Charalambos Filippousis (**19**), was also built in an L-shape, in two stages. The newest part is decorated in the same style as the older: friezes with rhombi are separated by one where suns and cypresses alternate. The upper friezes do not have any small openings, for easier access to the dovecote interior: it acts rather as a low wall that surrounds the roof. It is worth noting the decoration of the banquette.

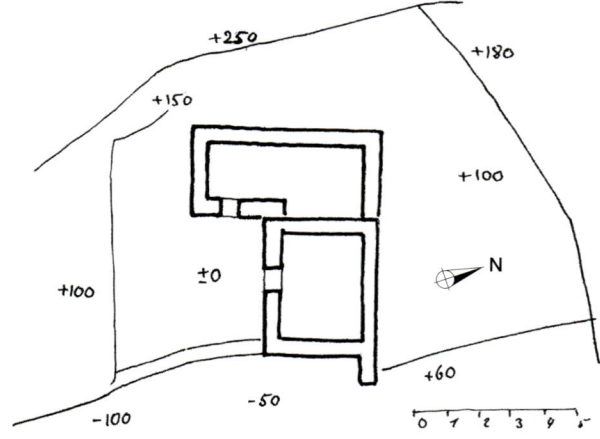

20 TARAMBADOS

This dovecote (**20**) recently passed into the hands of Fragkiskos Kritikos, from Triantaros. Old and charming, it is still plastered, but the roof has collapsed. For its reconstruction, the new owner vacillates between an old-style roof, which is more economical, and a concrete slab.

One of the banquettes, richly decorated, extends to the upper frieze, without small openings, with a simple wall around the roof. The corner columns continue up at the corners and onto the anta walls.

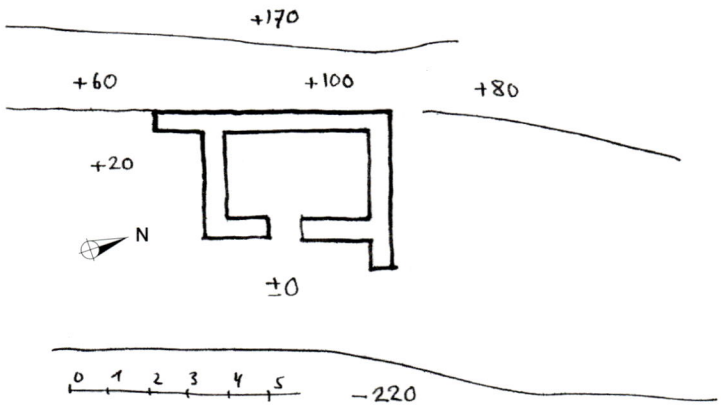

21 TARAMBADOS

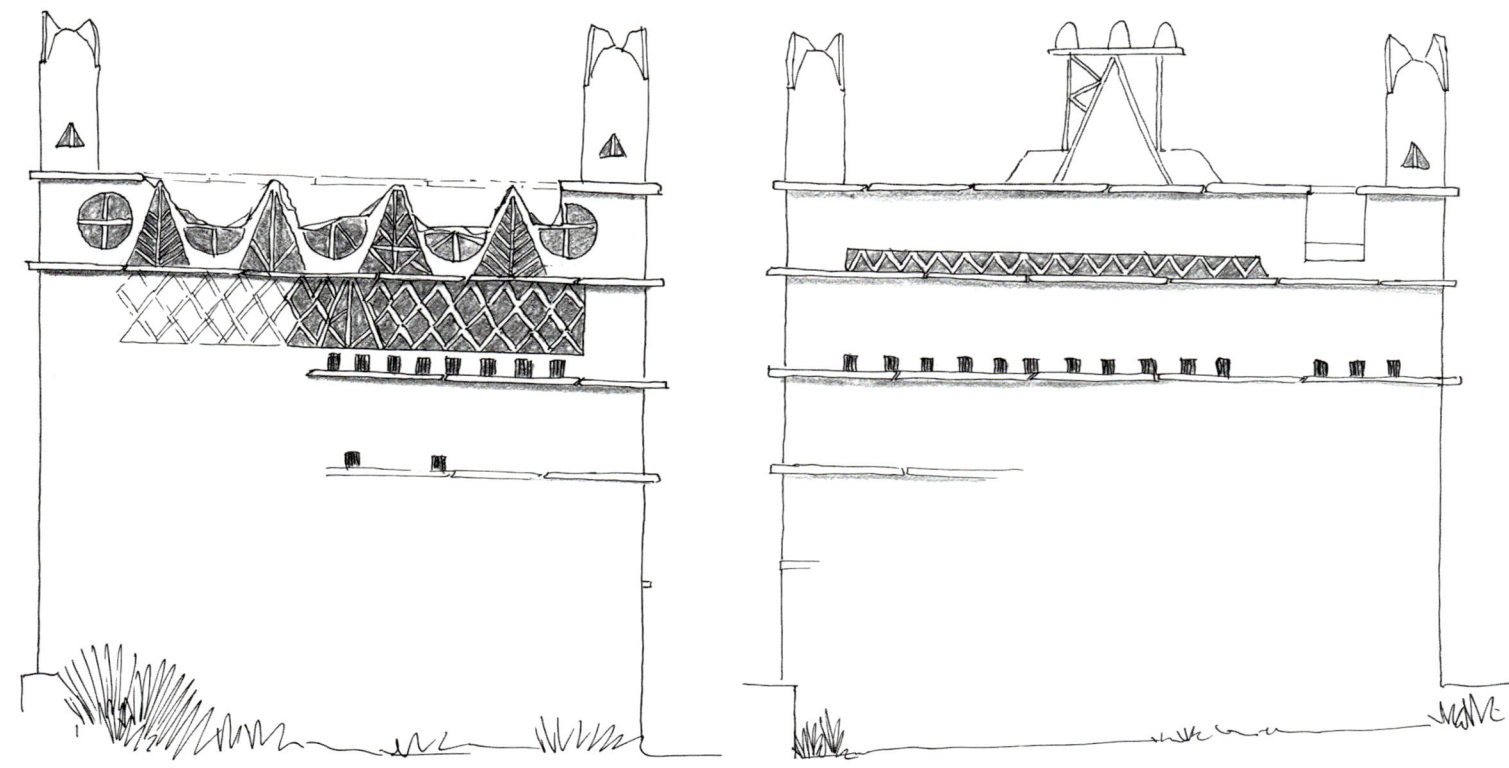

West facade

North facade

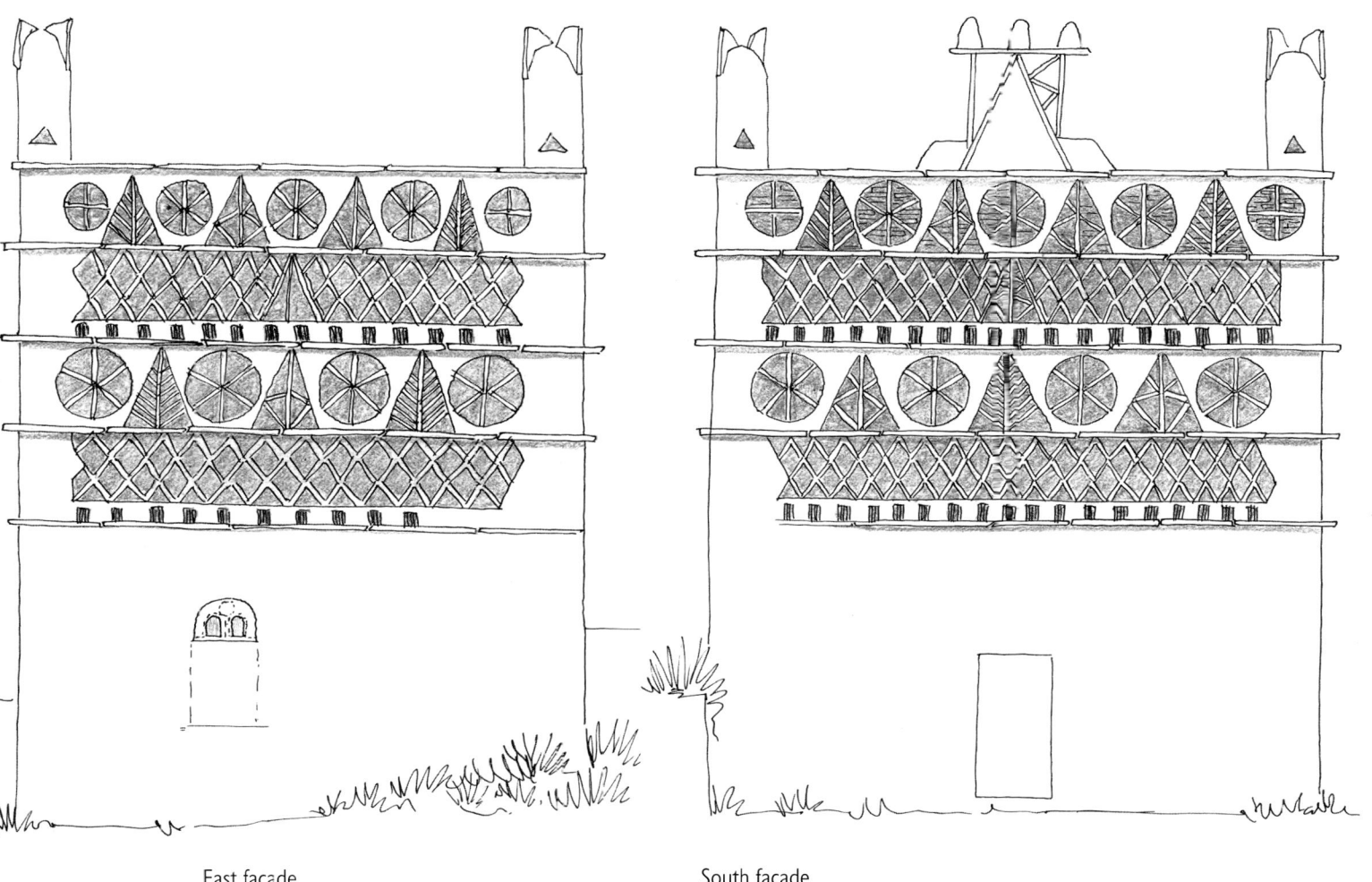

East facade

South facade

This very old, large dovecote (**21**) borders a stone path. Its two facades, the south and the west, are richly decorated and almost the same in appearance, with a banquette on the south facade, while a small carved marble slab is located above the built-in window on the east.

We can observe alternating cypresses and suns, from one horizontal frieze to another.
The upper frieze of the west facade, partially damaged, shows that its only function was to decorate the small wall that surrounds the terraced roof.

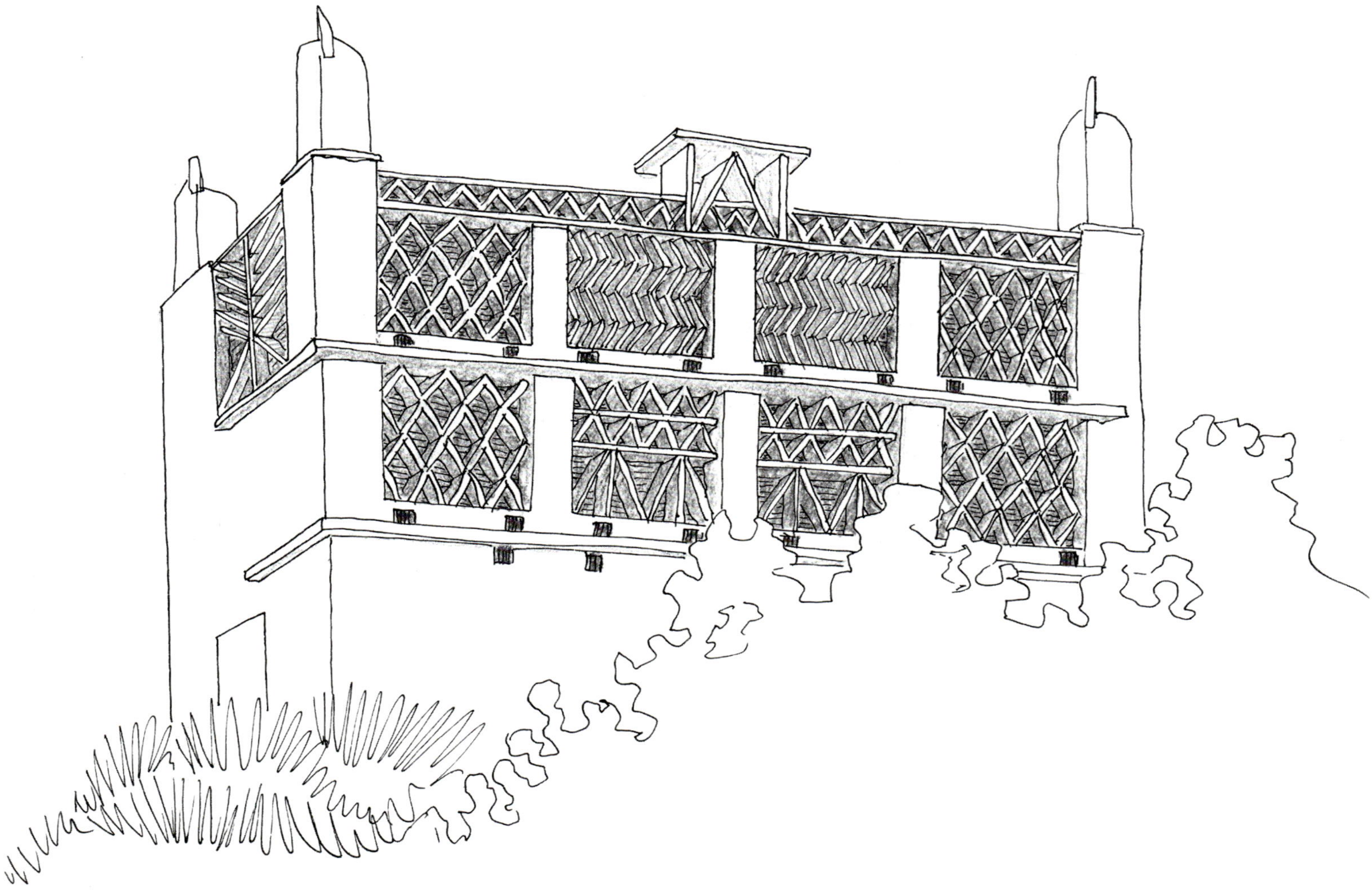

22 TARAMBADOS

We now follow the uphill path that passes in front of this dovecote and come to the one of Markos Delasouzas (**22**), built around 1945. It is very tall and thus stands out from the previous ones: the continuous friezes are replaced by many rectangular spaces, decorated with herringbone motifs and occasionally with two cypresses. A frieze with half rhombi decorates the low wall at the roof.

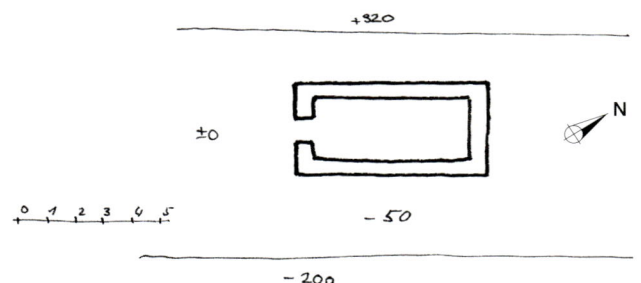

TARAMBADOS 23

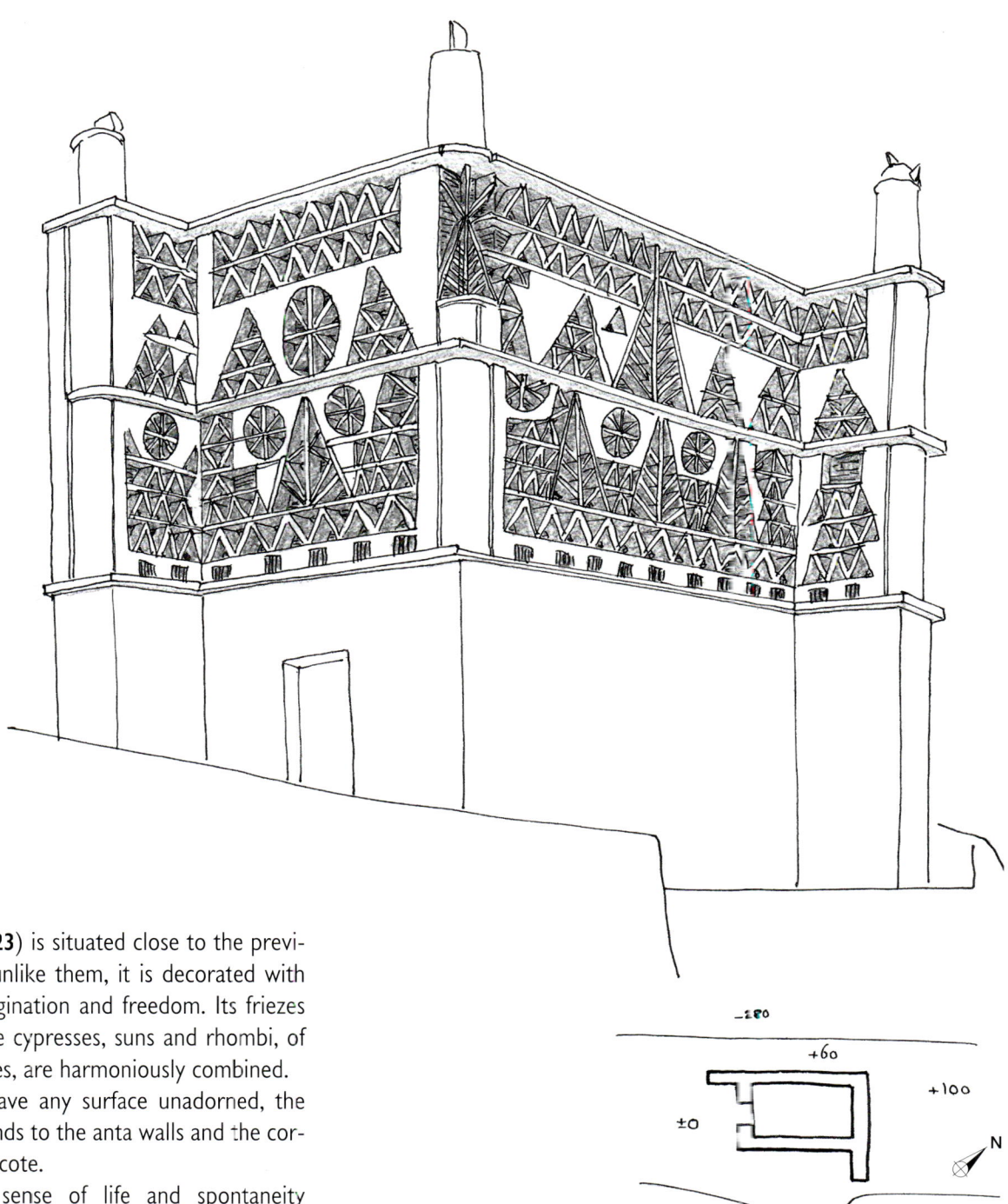

This dovecote (**23**) is situated close to the previous ones, but, unlike them, it is decorated with exceptional imagination and freedom. Its friezes are higher, while cypresses, suns and rhombi, of all kinds and sizes, are harmoniously combined.
So as not to leave any surface unadorned, the decoration extends to the anta walls and the corners of the dovecote.
An impressive sense of life and spontaneity emerges from this edifice.

24 AGIOS ROMANOS

From Agia Marina to Kardiani, between the road and the sea, there are numerous small valleys. Barren in their upper reaches, almost all have a spring or well near the sea. Olives, prickly pears, reeds and garden fruits grow there, as well as many dovecotes.

The beach below three of these small valleys is named after the chapel of Agios Romanos. The bay of Agios Romanos, one of the most beautiful beaches on the island, is tucked between two capes, one rounded like lava flow, the other sharpened like a blade. Between them, the bluish silhouette of Syros floats in the sea. Every morning, fishermen come to the beach with its fine sand to pull up their big brown net: the trawl. There are many dovecotes here. One of them (**24**) has an unusual roof, with a central pillar instead of a banquette.

BEFORE KARDIANI **25**

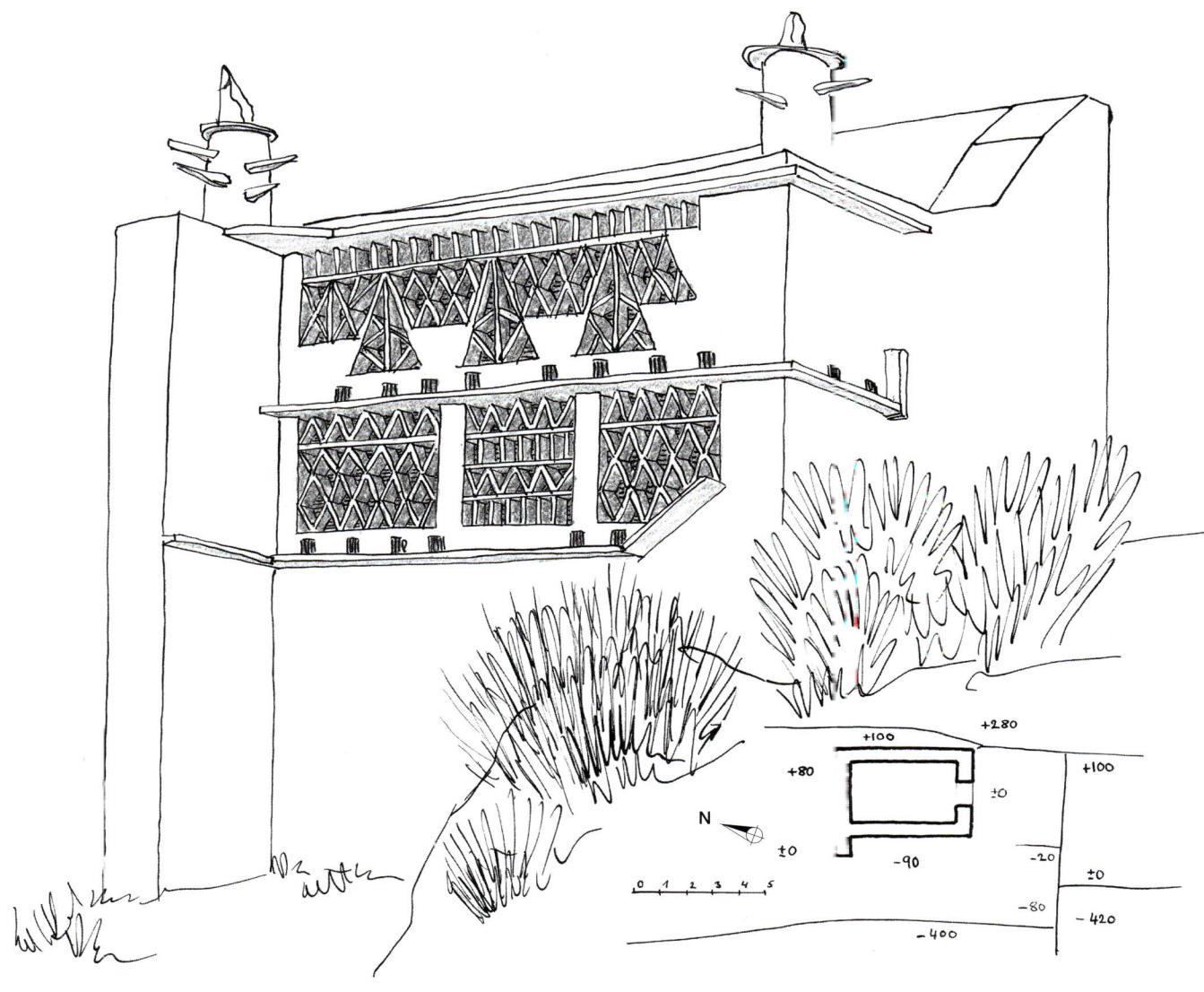

In a barren valley, before that of Kardiani, we may detect a large white chasm: an abandoned marble quarry.
I drew here a strange dovecote (**25**), old and extremely beautiful, half of which is still plastered.

Slate and marble were used in its construction. The decoration consists of three large cypress trees, rhombi, and a series of vertical slabs set around the roof. Two small, solid marble blocks are placed on the columns.

87

26 KARDIANI

East facade

West facade

KARDIANI, a most beautiful village, forms a semicircle above the olive trees. Once we cross the stream, we climb some wonderful stone stairs. Babbling water flows alongside them and on each wide landing there are marble basins, so that the mules and donkeys can quench their thirst.

Below the village, among the olive trees, is one of the most beautiful dovecotes in the village, owned by Antonios Lorenzos (**26**). It is worth noting the symmetry of the two side facades. On this dovecote alone there are four different types of cypresses to be seen.

South facade

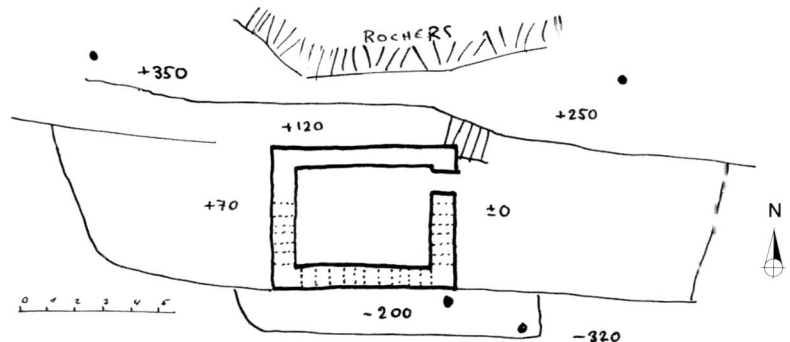

27 KARDIANI

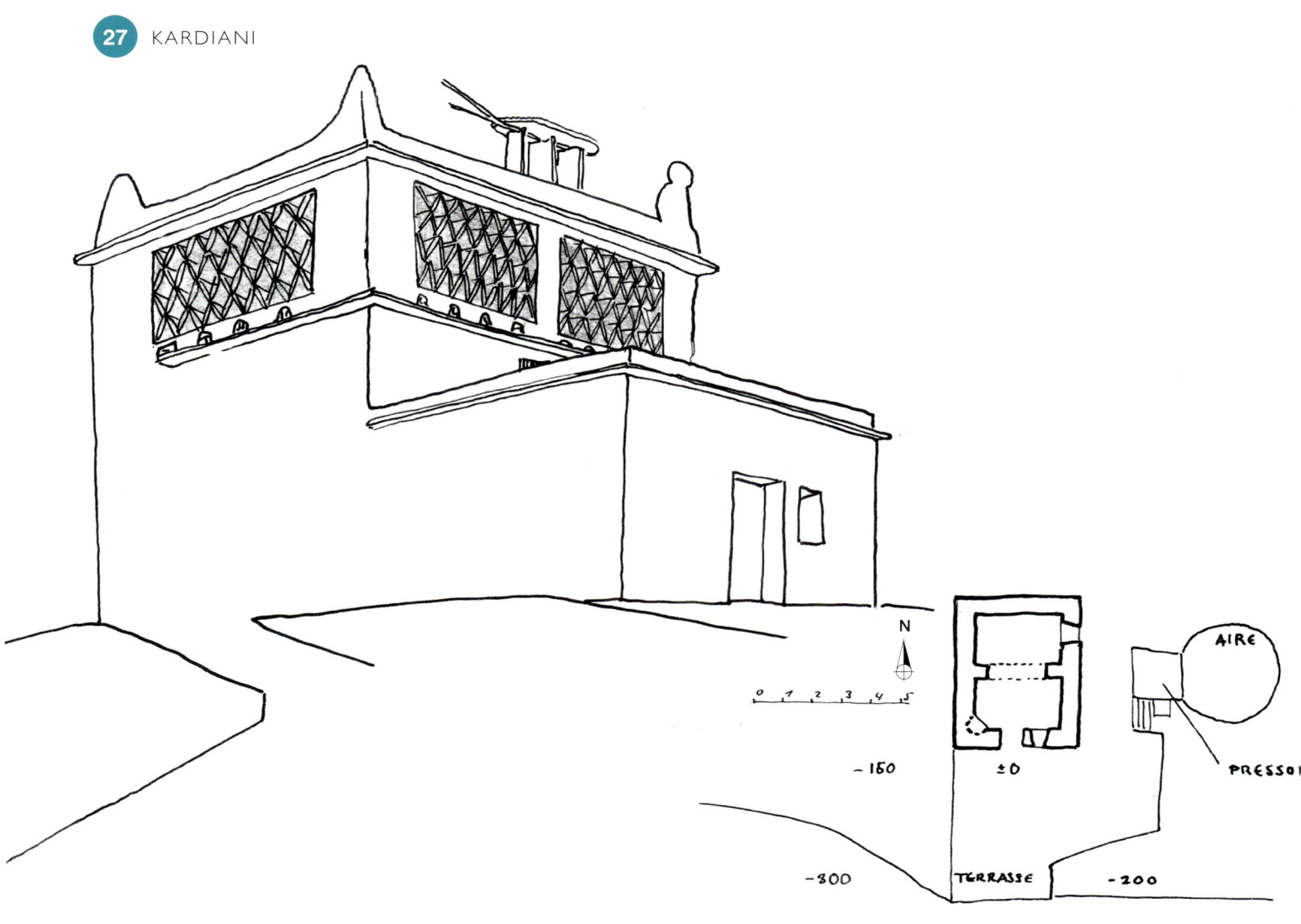

Descending the ravine, amidst the pink oleanders, we reach a beach where four dovecotes rise. That of Antonios Apergis (**27**) was built around 1890. Arriving there, I was dying of thirst. I heard a yellow dog barking and immediately Antonios appeared with a basket of grapes under his arm. He pushed me into the ground floor room, apologizing for the poverty inside: "Women do not come down here", he told me. I saw a fireplace, jars, sieves for wheat and a few sacks. It is one of those dovecotes that were built in fields, where people winnow the wheat and end up spending the night there. The room, like the dovecote, is covered with plaques, with slightly protruding walls. A stick is embedded in the banquette to scare off birds of prey, "like a rifle" (see Figs. 22 and 23, p. 47, for the interior).

KARDIANI 28

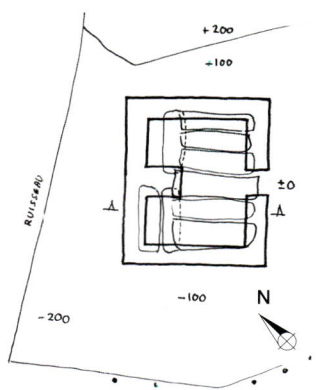
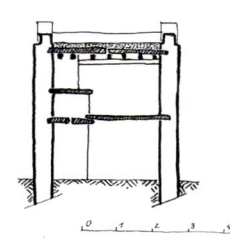

Below the village, is a dovecote (**28**) of particular interest. The interior is made of slate and marble slabs, and opposite the door there is an additional wall on which two large slabs rest. Thus, the other roofing slabs have a smaller surface to cover, as is shown in the drawing.

29 KARDIANI

The dovecote of Nikolaos Palamaris (**29**) is close to the previous one, and it too is made of marble. Its decoration consists of two central motifs, rare in the area, asymmetrically placed on both sides. The banquette has been replaced by two carved slabs. The left-hand one is called "bird" and is supposed to attract the pigeons, while the right one, which has a stranger shape, is called "cuckoo" and is there to scare off the birds of prey. That is at least the explanation given to me by the locals.

KARDIANI **30**

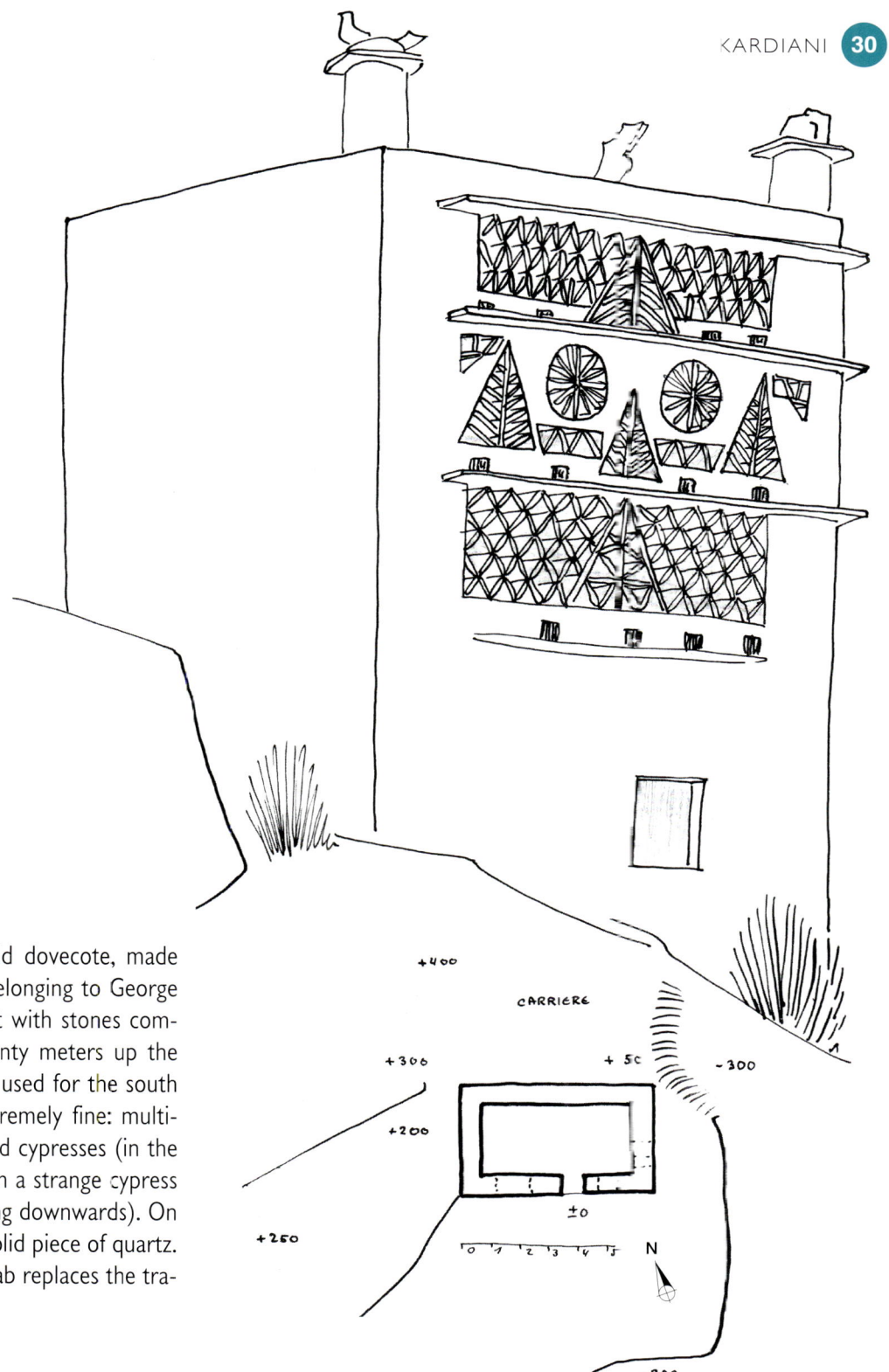

Very close by, there is an old dovecote, made of a slighty ferrous marble, belonging to George Kaloumenos (**30**). It was built with stones coming from a small quarry, twenty meters up the slope. The smaller ones were used for the south facade. The decoration is extremely fine: multi-rayed suns with many rays and cypresses (in the upper decoration there is even a strange cypress tree with the branches pointing downwards). On a column we see set a small solid piece of quartz. A simple irregularly-shaped slab replaces the traditional banquette.

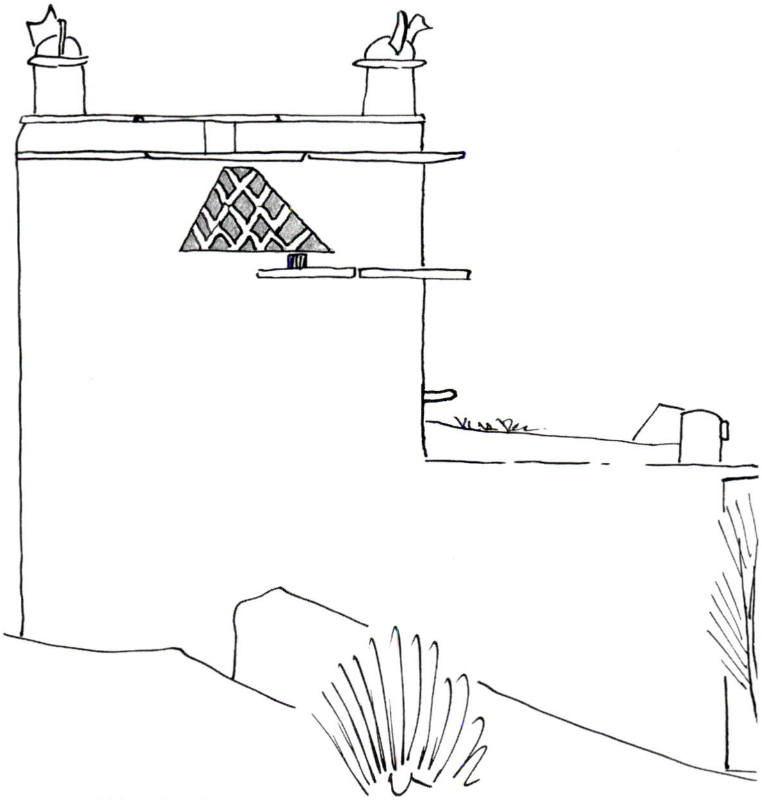

31 BEACH OF KARDIANI

West facade

East facade

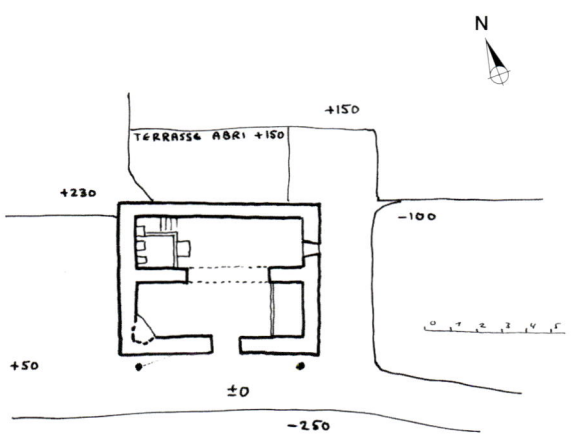

Remaining on the beach of Kardiani, we meet another charming dovecote (**31**), recently whitewashed. The ground floor includes a large room with a fireplace in one corner, and opposite is a slab placed on the edge, drilled with holes so that pieces of wood can be inserted and thus to set up beds. In the back there is a wine press. A hatch in the ceiling, above the press, gives direct access to the dovecote. There are about sixty small openings in its walls, extending from a protruding slab. Other nests sites are arranged in the corners (see Fig. 11 p. 31).

South facade

The decoration is very pleasant and rich. The false symmetry that dominates on both sides of the central motif creates an extremely vivid work. The central motif, a kind of hybrid sun-cypress, is very strange, as is the thin plaque occupying the traditional place of the banquette.

A large garden with a chapel stretches down to the beach, where every morning fishermen come to pull in their trawl nets. They exchange their fish for watermelons grown by the owner of the dovecote, who comes from a fairly remote village and prefers to spend his summer here with his family. But the noise of the humans presence drove away the pigeons.

The last village on the south coast is **YSTERNIA**. Anyone ascending from Kardiani comes upon the village suddenly, after passing a protruding rock. The village is very large, its roads are made up of marble stairs, and it has many churches. The most recent is beautifully decorated, with a complex marble iconostasis and two lions supporting the episcopal throne. An old woman told me to put my hand in their mouth to find that they "even have teeth". This is where the marble-bearing region begins. Near the village and running right up to the edge of the island there are huge quarries. But there are no springs, no vegetation and therefore no dovecotes!

Surprisingly, in an area that has so many craftsmen, the dovecotes in **YSTERNIA** — like those in Stasi, the small valley before it — are recent and of little interest. Often, they have only a few small openings, with no real decoration. Nevertheless, between the village and the sea, on the large rocks above the reeds of the ravine, there is a large, whitewashed dovecote (**32**). Its shape is complex. When pigeons are there, they occupy the upper floor, while in front, at level 0 on the floor plan, there is a room without a roof, whose wall is decorated with a frieze of half-rhombi. Below by 2.30 m, there is a large room which leads into a smaller room. Even further down, in a small shelter (at -3.80 m) with a sloping floor, I spent the night.

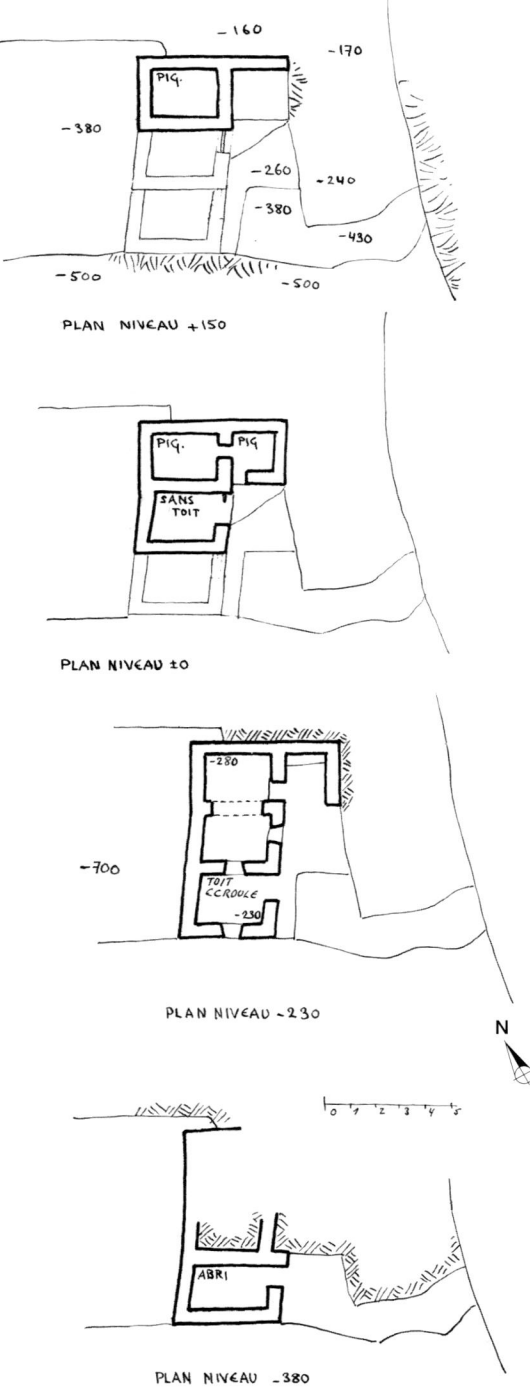

YSTERNIA 32

SECOND ROUTE

NORTHWEST PART OF THE ISLAND: EXO MERI AND KATO MERI

A river, the Kampas, which reaches the sea in the bay of Panormos, divides EXO MERI. The main town is Pyrgos. Further north, however, there are a few villages (Mamados, Marlas and Skamnidia), on a tributary of the Kampas. They are well protected from the north winds (as in the past from pirates), by a mountain range that, from east to west, overlooks the river.

With a few, rare exceptions, the little dovecotes in Exo Meri are relatively recent, made in a rough and ready manner, without any specific style. They often consist of mixed elements, sometimes with traces of colouring. Some of them may have been influenced by the large dovecotes built around the end of the 19th century in Kato Meri and which are separated only by a mountain mass from those in Exo Meri.

24. Picturesque stepped cobbled path (*kalderimi*) in Pyrgos. The main village of Exo Meri is one of the largest and most impressive on the island. On the hairpins of the road near Pyrgos is the dovecote (35) built of marble in 1941 (see drawing p. 106).

25. The dovecote (36) is located in the old village of Venardados, which today is part of Pyrgos, the centre of Exo Meri. Its decoration (see drawings pp. 107–109), consisting of rectangular shapes, is common in the area.

26. The dovecote with the huge initials Z. X. of the owner's name, belongs to the end of the 19th century (like 37, 38, 40, 43, 44 and 45) and has the features of what we would call "the Kato Meri style".

27.

27. The beautiful dovecote (56) to the south of the village of Smardakito, is characterized by the columns that are inserted in the overlapping horizontal zones of the decoration in slate (see drawings on pp. 132–133).

28. The old dovecote (47) is located at the top of the valley that descends to Kato Kleisma, near the chapel of Agia Marina, on the road leading from Kampos to Kardiani (see drawings pp. 122–123).

33 MAMADOS

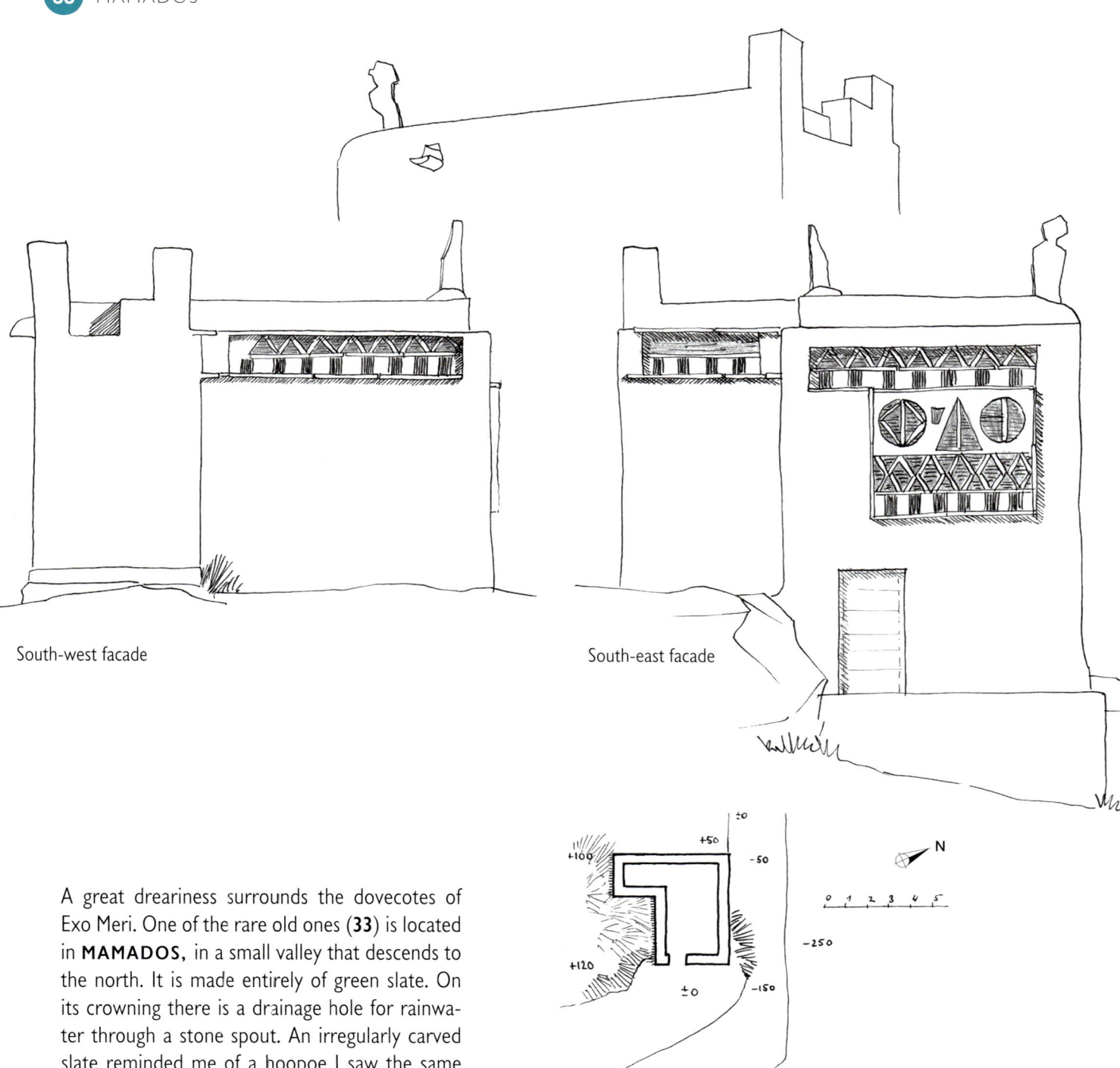

South-west facade

South-east facade

A great dreariness surrounds the dovecotes of Exo Meri. One of the rare old ones (**33**) is located in **MAMADOS,** in a small valley that descends to the north. It is made entirely of green slate. On its crowning there is a drainage hole for rainwater through a stone spout. An irregularly carved slate reminded me of a hoopoe I saw the same morning in Steni.

Near **MARLAS**, in the small valley of Banikas, Formosis Xypolitidis from Pyrgos owns a dovecote (**34**) that was built about thirty years ago. It is made of marble and slate.

The crowning consists of marble slabs. On them are bell-shaped columns. The three letters that stand out are the initials of the name of the father of the current owner: Ioannis Georgiou Xypolitidis. The whole dovecote is covered with white plaster, but in some places the plaster is painted bright blue. The marble cross, shown in the drawing, was placed for decorative purposes on the wall built in front of the dovecote.

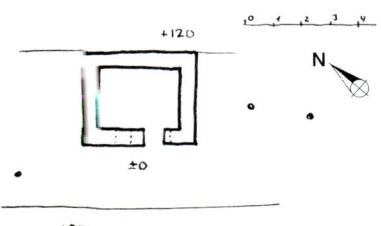

35 PYRGOS

The valley of Marlas ends in the deep, and now very nearby, bay of Panormos, where I did not spot any dovecotes. From this bay, another valley stretches southeast to Pyrgos (today Panormos), Venardados and, finally, to Ysternia. On the hairpins in the road, near **PYRGOS**, we find another dovecote (**35**), built like the previous ones, without a clear plan. It is made only of marble, but plastered everywhere and shows traces of colouring in places. At its top there are marble decorations, and between the small openings of the upper frieze, under a banquette carved from a solid piece of marble, a plaque bears the inscription: "BUILT BY THE BROTHERS KALOGRIAI 1941".

There are other dovecotes in the village, some more recent like the previous two, others casually adjoined to a house: none however are of particular interest.

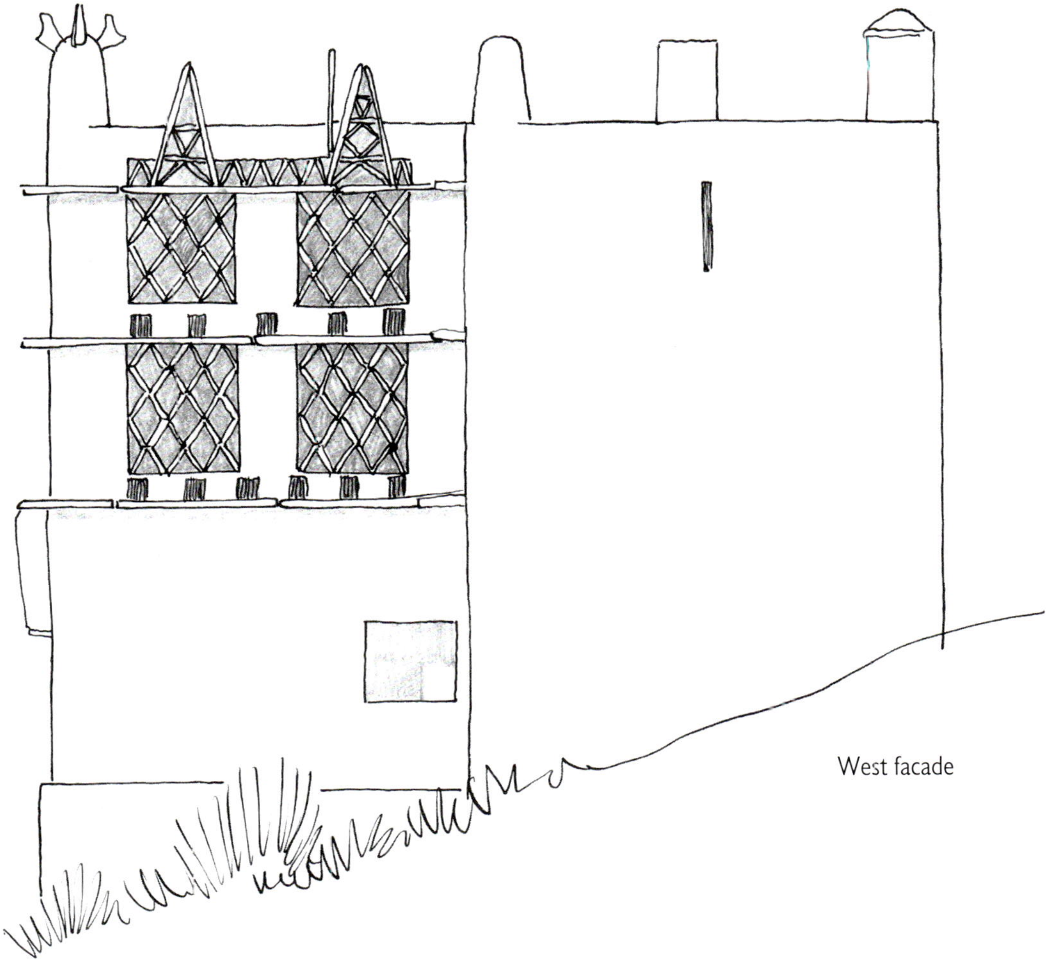

VENARDADOS 36

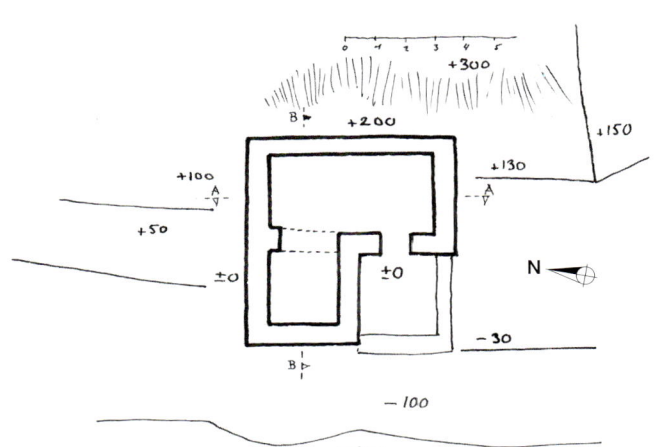

West facade

The village of **VENARDADOS** is essentially now a part of Pyrgos, which is the main village in Exo Meri. On the opposite slope of the valley is the most beautiful dovecote in the area (**36**) (see Fig. 25, p. 100).

On the way to Steni, I had already noticed, from high up on the mountain, its large L-shaped terraced roof, covered with clay of a bright orange hue. The decoration of the dovecote was executed

36 VENARDADOS

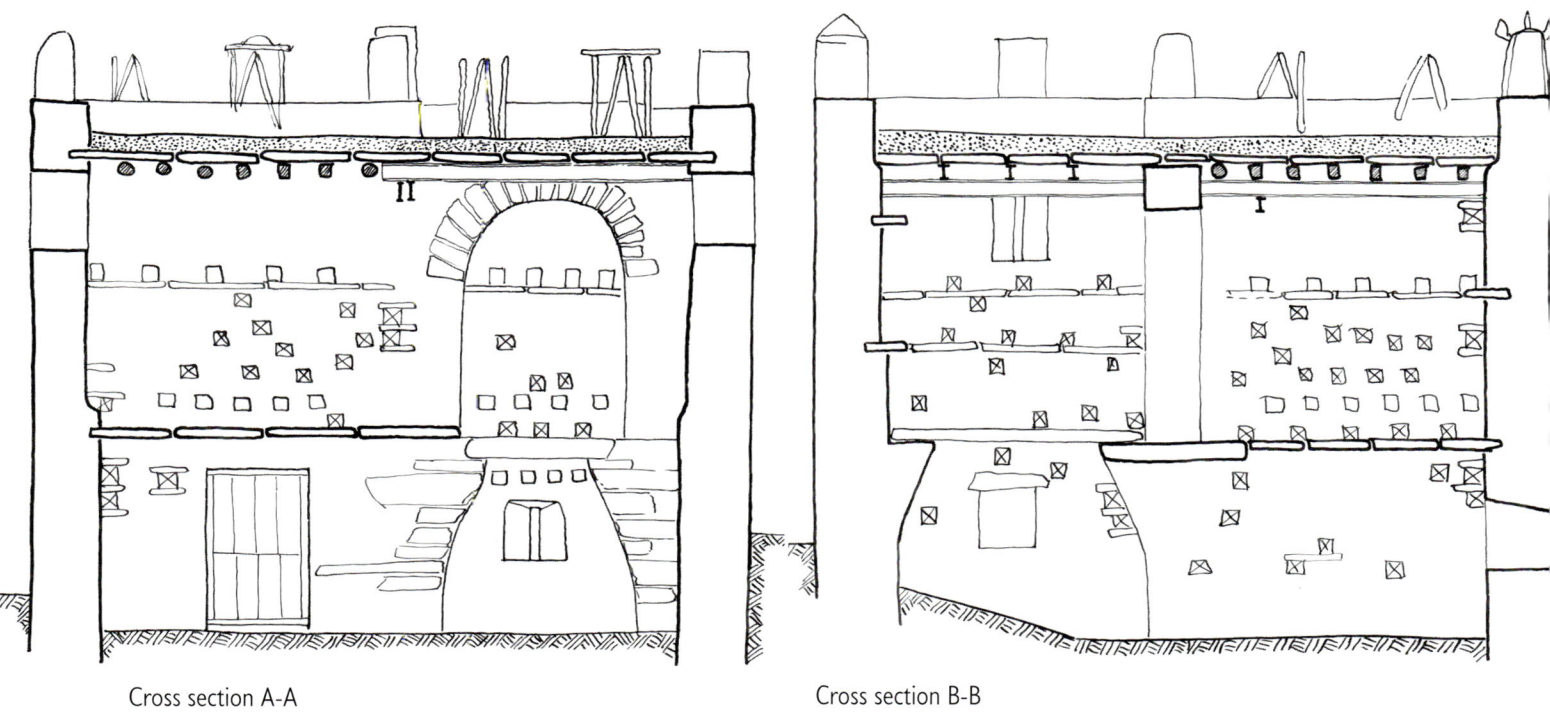

Cross section A-A

Cross section B-B

with simplicity and care: on each facade there are four rectangular sections full of rhombi. The crowning includes a row of half rhombi and two banquettes on each facade. On the front of the entrance, high up and on the right, there is a marble slab with the inscription: 1843 SEPT | EMBER 1 | IAKOBOS | PERANTA | KOS.

In the two drawn sections, we can appreciate its interior. The nests, simple ones without a slab, are indicated by an x. We make the total 170! We also see in the west wing the detail of the roof, formed by slabs resting on beams or irons. The middle floor consists of slabs, mounted on walls with a large protruding edge.

South facade

109

37 KALLONI

A mountain mass, not very high but uninhabited, which extends north from the main mountain range of the island, separates, as we have seen, **EXO MERI** (in the west) from **KATO MERI** (in the east). Small wild valleys descend to the north and to the sea. In one of them, Skoteino Lagkadi (The dark meadow), there are a few dovecotes.

The centre of Kato Meri consists of a large plain, which ends in the bay of Kolimbithra. Above the bay, the villages of Karkados (now integrated into Kalloni), Kato Kleisma and Aetofolia are clustered around some springs — in a place where seafarers cannot see them, as in the past the pirates never spotted them either.

The slopes surrounding these villages are sparsely cultivated, as the neighbouring plain provides more fertile plots of land. All around there are many dovecotes dating from the end of the 19th century, in a completely different style from those we have described so far.

One of them (**37**) is located above the stream, very close to **KALLONI**, and is completely plastered and whitewashed, except for the ground floor. It belongs to Marco Armaos.

It is inhabited by many pigeons. It is made according to the distinctive stylistic rules of Kato Meri. One of the facades, very richly decorated, acquires thereby a prominence, so we can talk about the main facade and side facades.

The decoration no longer consists of horizontal friezes: the main facade is divided by pilasters, to its entire height, into three parts. Most rhombi have been replaced by vertical slabs that support thin horizontal plaques.

The initials of the owner's name and the date of construction, which stand out against the slabs, were created from mudbricks and plastered. An ornamental flower made in the same way occupies the centre of the composition.

The crowning creates a very rich, intricate ensemble, and on top there are small pediments.

38 KALLONI

On the far bank of the river, the dovecote of Lorenzos Armaos (**38**) stands opposite to the previous one, positioned to overlook the sunset, to do which required the construction of a small anta wall.
It is in the same style as the previous dovecote, but the decoration of the facade consists exclusively of slabs (except for a zone of rhombi). We see the engraved initials L. Z .A.: was he the grandfather of the current owner? In the centre of the decoration of the side facade, between two cypress trees, set in very large rectangles, there is a small decorative pattern in the shape of a fan.
The crowning occupies a large area, as in the previous example. At the corners and next to the pilasters stand small square pillars, crowned with built-in stone hemispheres, which are filled in with slate fragments.
The roofing was made with slabs supported on wooden beams and then covered with a layer of soil.

39 KALLONI

Still in **KALLONI**, but a little higher up, there is a garden surrounded by a high wall. Its owner, Rokos Armaos, had me taste all its fruits, peaches, pears, lemons, and even the aroma of the basil planted near the well.

In the middle of this garden, rises an old dovecote (**39**), which is completely plastered and whitewashed. In the drawing we see its south corner, with the two exposed facades. On the southwest facade, a staircase gives access to the terraced roof. The pigeons occupy only the upper floor, the lower one serves as a storeroom.

The dovecote is set in the middle of the garden, so all four facades are visible. This may be the reason why part of the decoration continues on the two northern facades, but with small decorative openings, which do not give access to the interior.

KALLONI **40**

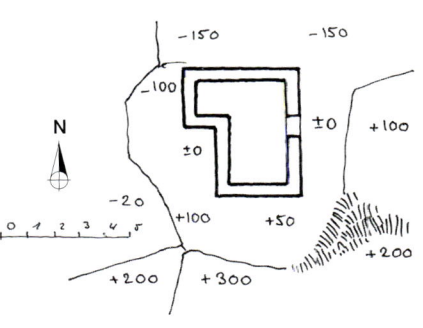

At a short distance from the above, but outside the irrigated zone, is an L-shaped dovecote (**40**) which belongs to Antonios Steriotis. This design dictates relatively narrow facades, which cannot be divided by pilasters. The decoration, however, is in the same style as the previous examples: with plaques, the initials of the owner's name, the date of construction (1891) and the tall cypress tree. However, the crowning is different. The whole dovecote is plastered and whitewashed, except for the decoration of the slabs.

41 KARKADOS

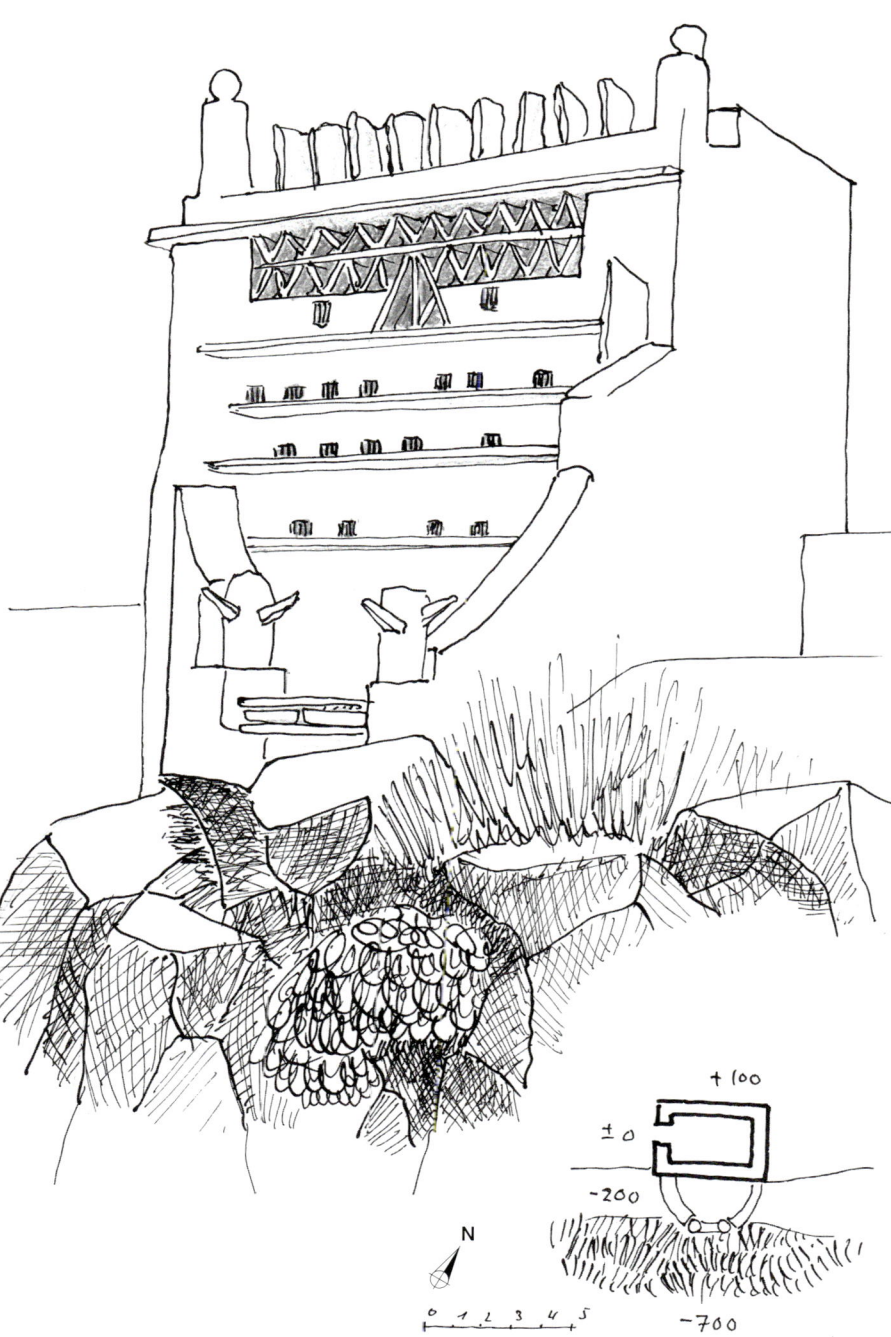

Opposite Kalloni, the small village of **KARKADOS** counts four dovecotes looking to the south, on the steep bank of the stream that separates the village from Kalloni. None of these dovecotes have any links to the style favoured in Kato Meri. The dovecote (**41**), which belongs to Donados Armaos, is of particular interest. Small in size, plastered, except for the background of the decoration, it has only a few small openings in the facade and a frieze of rhombi. However, two rounded walls with two columns at the ends surround a lower terrace supported by a protruding rock. Whatever the reason for this, the arrangement gives the dovecote a very original character, which is emphasized by the upright plates on the crowning.

Another dovecote (**42**), in a similar position to the previous one, belongs to Giannis Armaos. It is characterized by the very uneven height of the various friezes: two rows of half rhombi frame a frieze in the middle, which is unusually high and clearly designed. It consists only of rhombi, with the exception of three cypresses. The dovecote is plastered and its doorstep is one meter above the ground.

KARKADOS 42

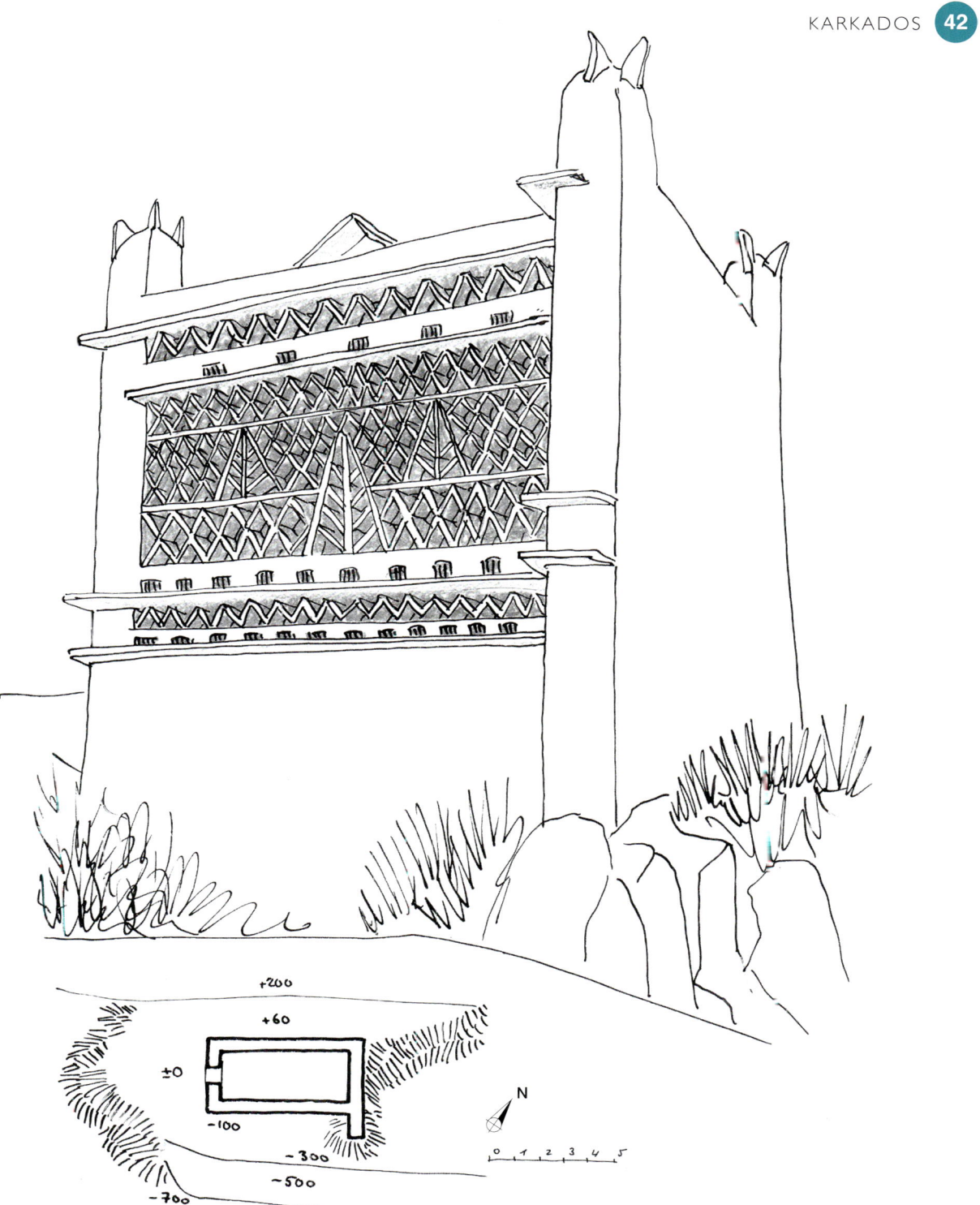

117

43 KATO KLEISMA

Near the village of **KATO KLEISMA** there are four dovecotes. Before I even saw them, one of them had been lauded to me as the most beautiful on the island. It has, at least, the richest decoration (**43**). It belongs to Ieremias Steriotis, from Kalloni, and is a nice example of the Kato Meri style. It dates from the late 19th century, is completely plastered and whitewashed; it looks like a huge, white, multi-layered cake. It was built with great care, while the precision of the decoration is also remarkable. On the main facade, which is decorated with rhombi and squares, there is a cross and the initials N. K. We may notice in the cornice a generously decorated banquette and below it a kind of crown built in the slabs.

As in all dovecotes of this style, the side facades are treated very differently, with two narrow cypresses set in high rectangles.

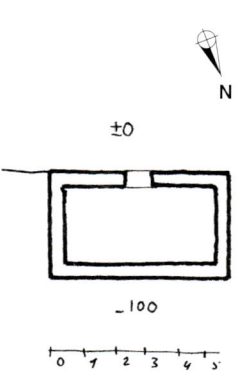

AETOFOLIA **44**

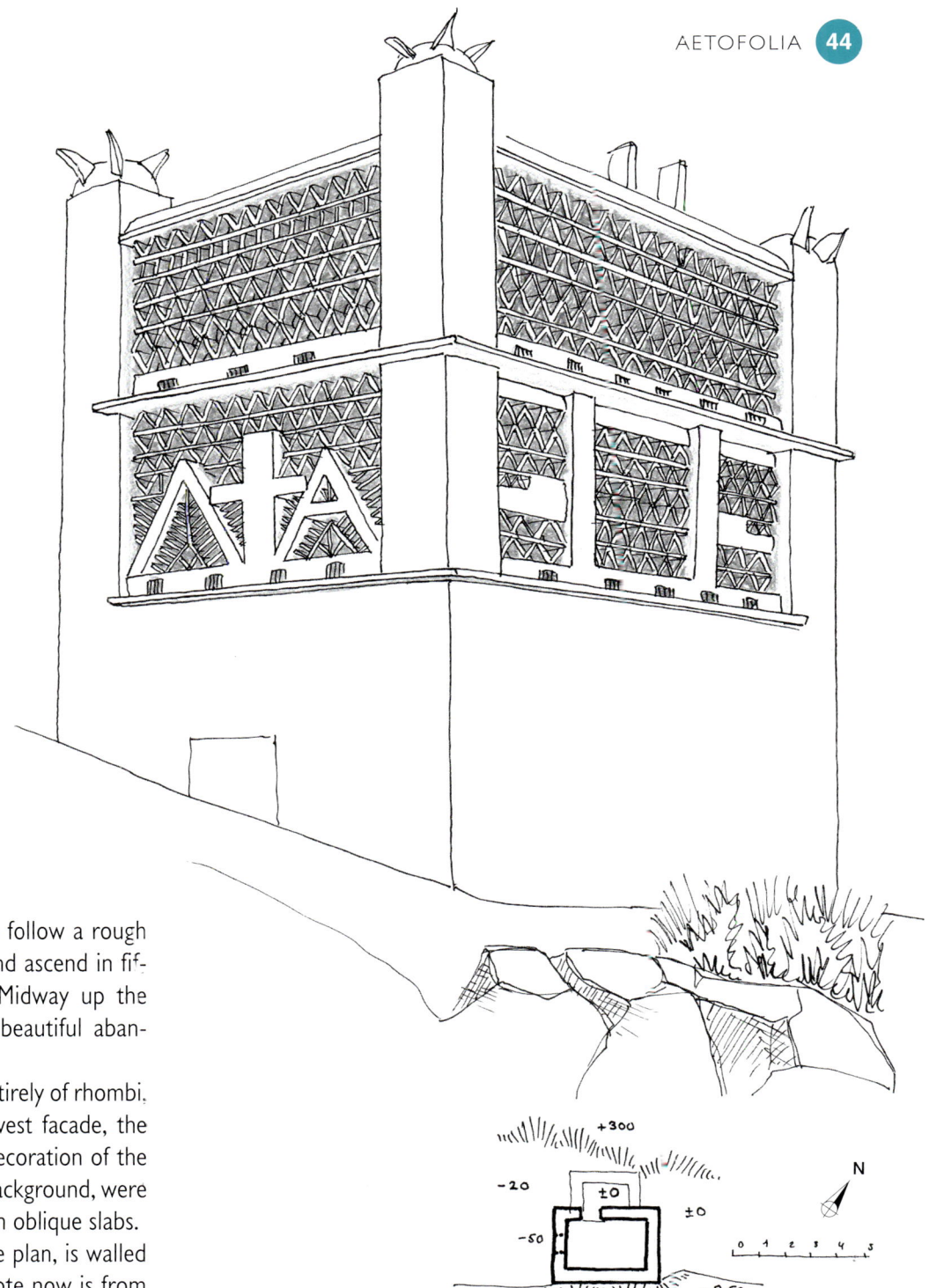

Leaving behind these villages, we follow a rough path that climbs a steep slope, and ascend in fifteen minutes to **AETOFOLIA**. Midway up the road, near a chapel, there is a beautiful abandoned dovecote (**44**).

Its decoration, made up almost entirely of rhombi, is extremely elaborate. On the west facade, the initials L. A. frame a cross. The decoration of the letters and their inclusion to the background, were skilfully done, with the help of thin oblique slabs. The southwest door, visible in the plan, is walled up, as the entrance to the dovecote now is from the upper floor, on the northwest facade.

45 VALLEY OF PLOMARI

Between Aetofolia and the sea, the narrow valley of **PLOMARI** is formed, tucked between very steep, gravelly slopes. Only at the lower part are there a few olive-trees. On the north side of the small valley, many dovecotes succed one another, most of them are very simple, some more richly decorated, many in the same style as seen in Kato Meri.

One of them (**45**), dates from 1894 and bears the initials Α.Σ. Again, we meet the decorative elements (herringbones, vertical slabs) and the typical arrangement of Kato Meri, namely mainly set in a rectangle, framed by tall cypresses, which enclose a rhombus. We also notice the large carved slab, undoubtedly anthropomorphic, located above the recessed corner of the dovecote.

KATRACHIANA 46

In the main part of the valley, between the sea and Komi, there is an important tributary stream, which descends from the highest peak of the island. This tributary is formed near the chapel of Agia Marina, and also at the point where the road of Komi is separated from that of the southern part of the island. The valley it creates is almost uninhabited, with the exception of the small village of **KATRACHIANA** at its upper part. There are still two chapels and four dovecotes. One of them (**46**) has rounded columns at the corners and strange stone frames around the lace-like slabs and the rayed half-suns. Two half-columns protrude above the door and frame a decoration with an arched top, which combines rhombi, slabs and a half-sun.

47 KATRACHIANA

South facade

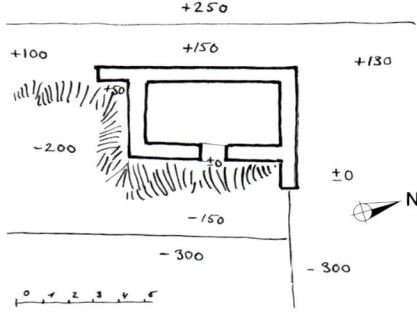

High up in the same valley, we see an old, very nice dovecote (**47**). It is related in style to those of Smardakito, which are not that far away. Here, too, the decoration is not organized in horizontal friezes. Elongated decorated spaces run in succession and sometimes at the top there is a sun or a semicircular arch occupied by a "half-sun" motif. The decorative design of the main banquette is also unusual (see also Fig. 28, p. 103)

East facade

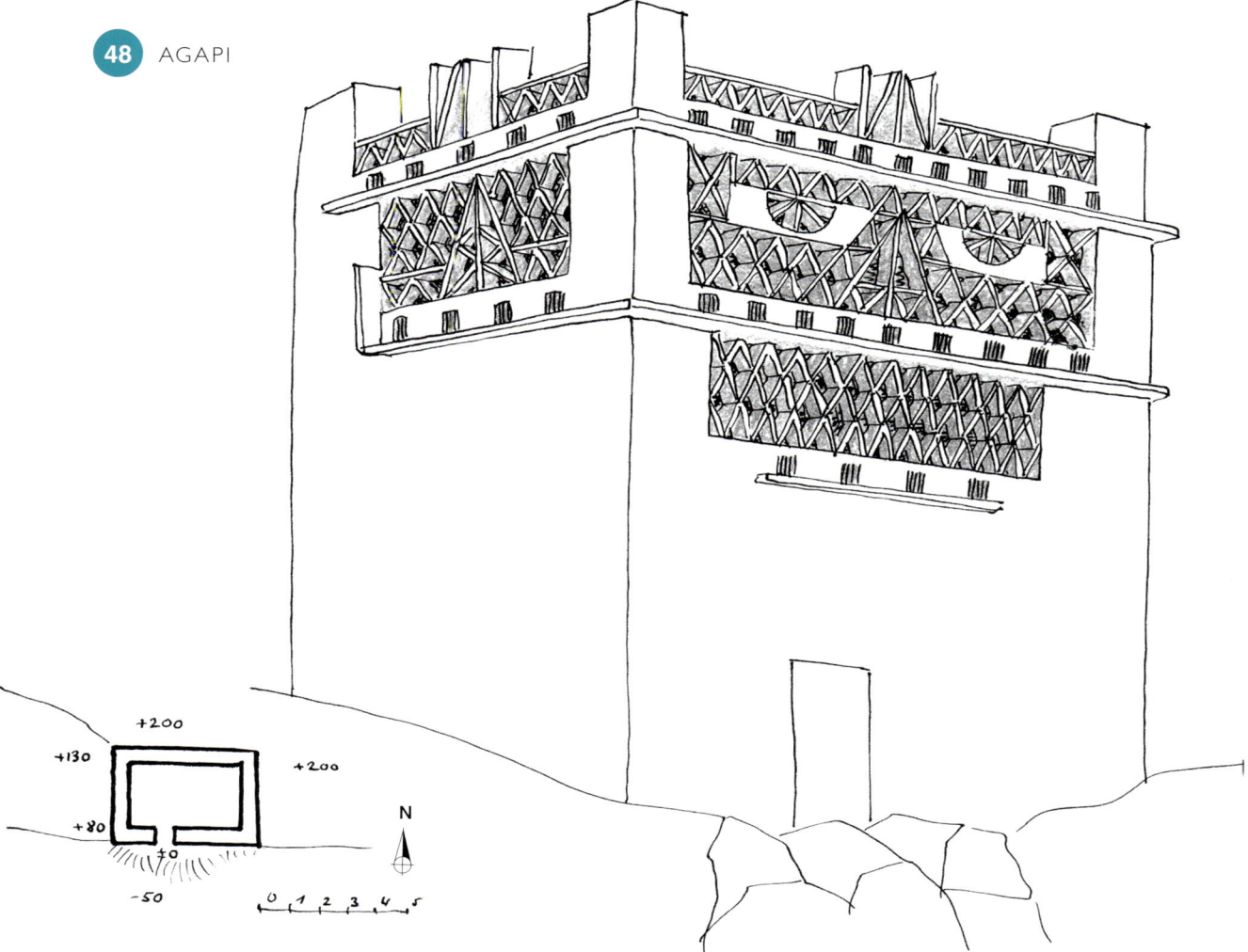

48 AGAPI

Another important valley ends in the plain of Kato Meri. It starts from the centre of the island, almost from the upland plateau of Steni, whose villages we will present later. The village **AGAPI**, which is the last, is situated just above the plain of Kato Meri. We reach it from the plain, walking along the river. Soon, many dovecotes and the houses of the village appear. The small valley that rises behind the spring, towards the north, is irrigated quite well. A fertile garden with two small dovecotes belongs to the nuns. Higher up, a few minutes away, at a spot called Pyrgos, two beautiful old dovecotes stand quite close to a small spring.

The first of them (**48**) belongs to Eleftherios Delatolas. It has nice proportions and is decorated with restraint and balance. The crowning consists of a series of small openings and on top there is a frieze with a series of half-rhombi. In the central frieze there stand out, on either side of the central cypress, two half-suns, surrounded by carefully plastered masonry. Above, there are again half-rhombi.

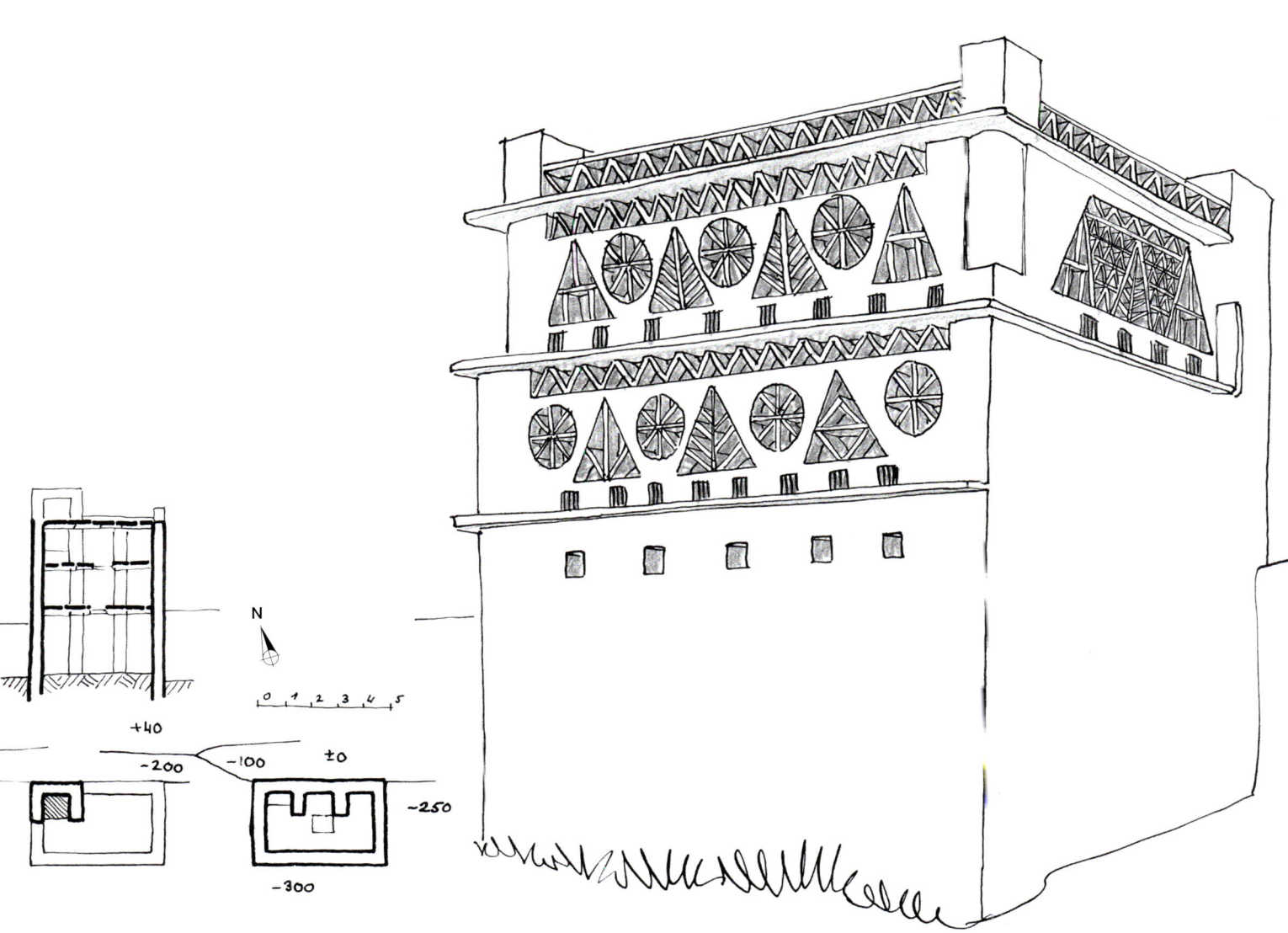

The other dovecote (**49**) is abandoned, partially plastered and open on three sides: it has a main facade on the south and two identical side faces. The side decoration is set in a trapezoidal outline and presents a harmonious symmetry with an elegant alternation of suns and cypresses, the latter in three different types.

The two mezzanine floors and the roof consist of large slabs. Some of them are supported on low internal retaining walls and thus cover a space larger than their individual dimensions. Access to this dovecote is only from the terraced roof, which has in one corner a small trapdoor, itself covered by small roofing (see section), which goes down to the ground floor.

50 AGAPI

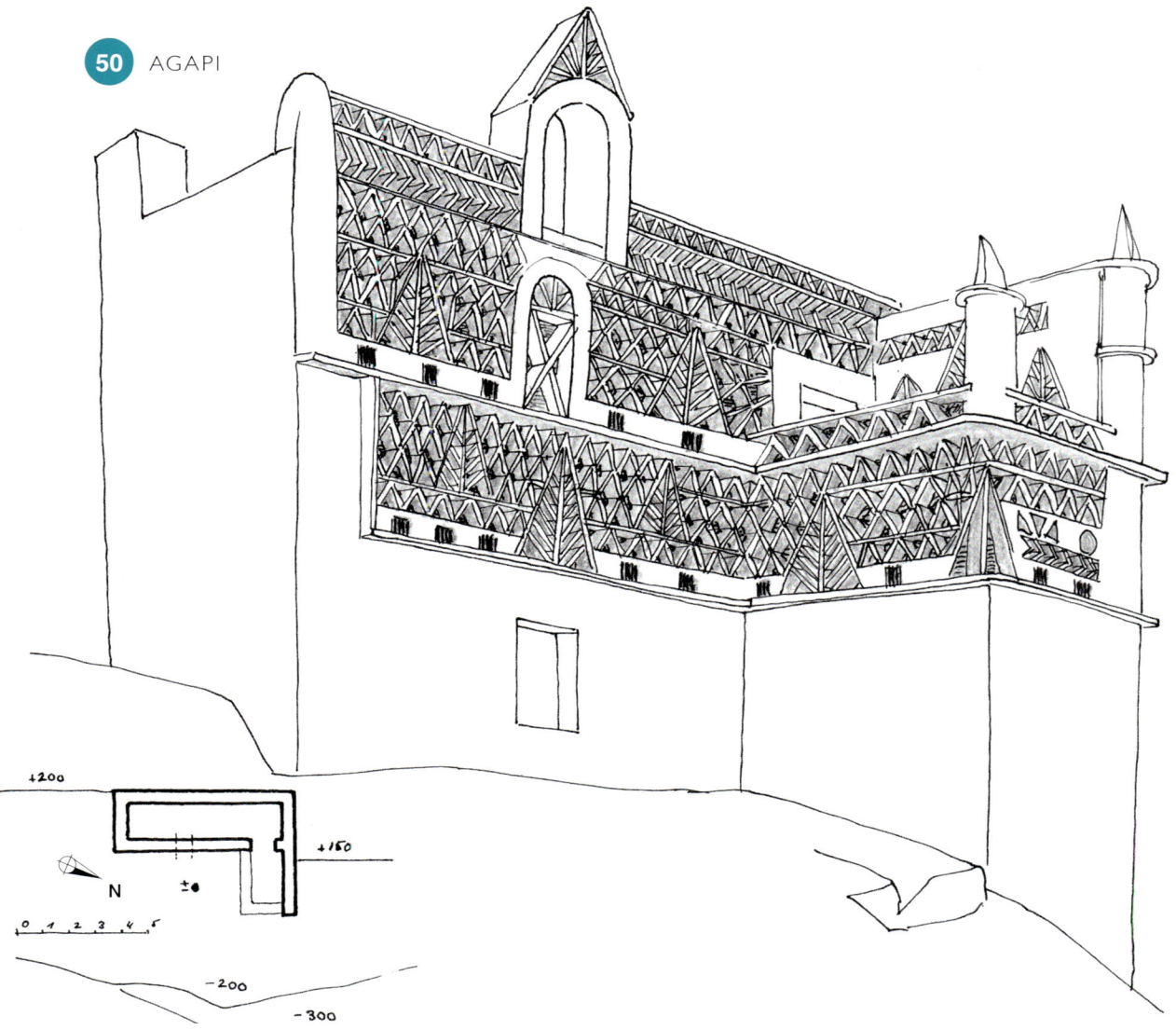

From the village of **AGAPI** rises another small valley, heading south. Its steep slopes are dry and yellowed. Just opposite the village, there are two dovecotes. They both demonstrate a very special local style. They are open only on one side and are extended out to the right by a large anta wall, of some size, on which rests a small porch, the height of which does not reach even half way up the dovecote.

One dovecote, very old, belongs to the local priest Stefanos (**50**). Because it has a shallow depth, slate slabs for the roof and floor were easily used. One door leads to a room on the ground floor and another door, on the flat roof of the porch, leads to the main dovecote. The decoration is very rich, consisting of cypresses, rhombi and a row of herringbone. We may observe the corner cypress, the central motif surrounded by a semicircular niche, and the stone banquette made in a new style.

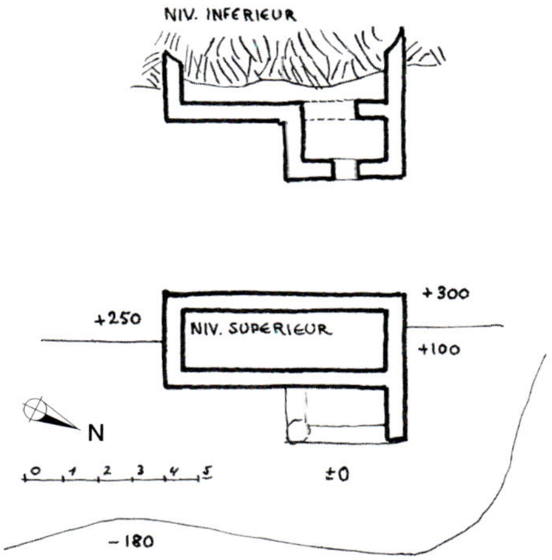

AGAPI 51

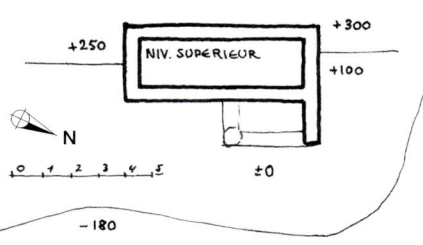

The other dovecote (**51**) is also old, with a similar porch at ground floor. It was decorated, however, with more moderation and discipline, almost entirely with rhombi. An arch connects the porch to the main part of the dovecote, while the natural rock almost completely encloses its lower part. Here, too, the narrowness of the construction facilitated the use of slate slabs.

52 AGAPI

Higher up, the valley is divided into two smaller, wild and desert valleys. In a large, fenced garden is an old, imposing dovecote (**52**), belonging to Stefanos Delatolas. The upper frieze is placed in a recess, as are the two banquettes on the main facade, with one higher than the other.

The decoration is quite symmetrical: a frieze with suns and cypresses, between two more with rhombi. It presents many interesting details, such as the design of the banquettes, or the variety of cypresses with intricate designs, sometimes with down-turned branches, framed by small inverted triangles. The west facade is not decorated. The roof is supported by wooden beams.

We leave, however, the valley of Agapi, to descend again to Komi.

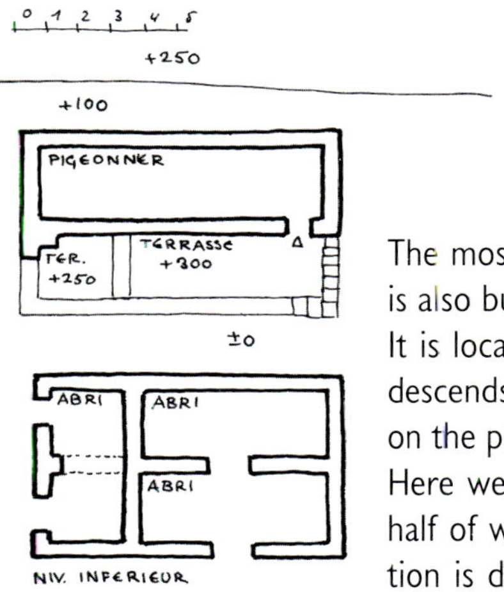

KOMI **53**

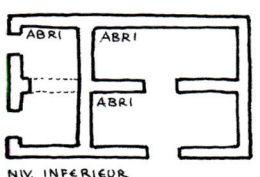

The most important village in Kato Meri, **KOMI**, is also built adjacent the large plain of Kato Meri. It is located on the left bank of the river, which descends from Loutra and Xynara and ends up on the plain.

Here we find an old, abandoned dovecote (**53**), half of whose plaster has fallen off. The decoration is designed freely, with cypresses, suns and rhombi. Above, there is a wide pediment, with a strange cypress in the centre.

Access to the terraced roof is facilitated by a staircase built into the anta wall. The roof consists of slate slabs, supported on beams and covered with clay soil. The floor also consists of slate slabs, the largest I have seen on the island: they reach 2.25 m in length.

54 PERASTRA

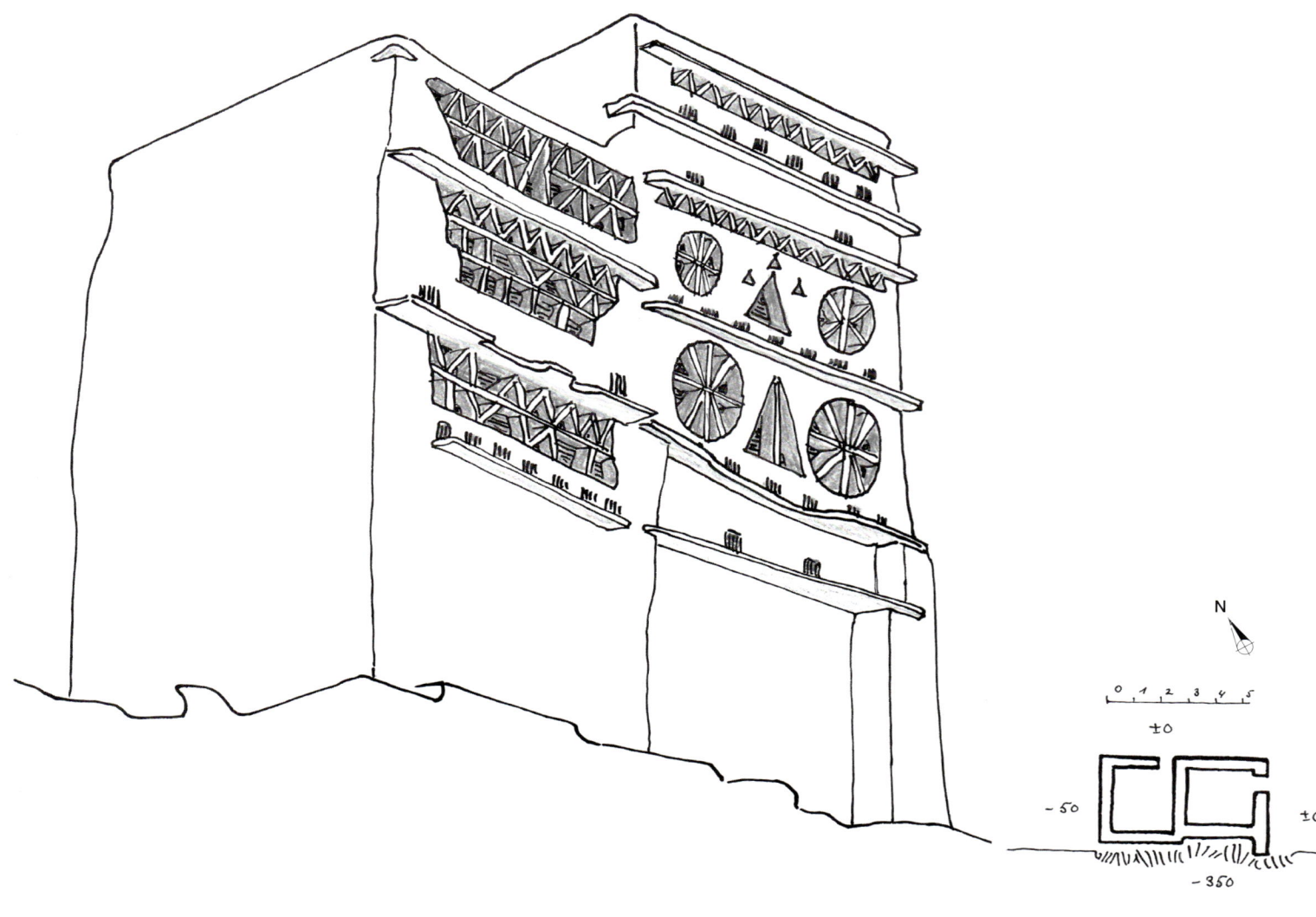

Ten minutes are enough to climb up again, following the line of the river, from Komi to **PERASTRA**, the next village. To our right, we meet a few dovecotes. One of them consists of two adjoining dovecotes (**54**). It is quite old, but still plastered, decorated very freely, without any resemblance between its two parts. The ratio of volumes — decorated surfaces with those that remained undecorated — is extremely successful.

There are other dovecotes around Komi, many of which were recently built. One of them abuts a house; another, typical of Kato Meri, bears the initials L. and K., with a cross and a vase.

A little further off from **PERASTRA**, a small fertile valley hosts an olive grove, gardens, and many dovecotes. One of them (**55**) is a typical example of dovecotes that are far off from the villages. It is built near a spring, which gushes out from under a domed structure. The water passes through a small channel cut into the stone, flows into a carved basin, and thence into a large tank. The dovecote is located in a corner of the enclosure. The decoration is very simple, with a few suns wedged into the stonework. The crowning is topped by two banquettes.

56 BELOW SMARDAKITO

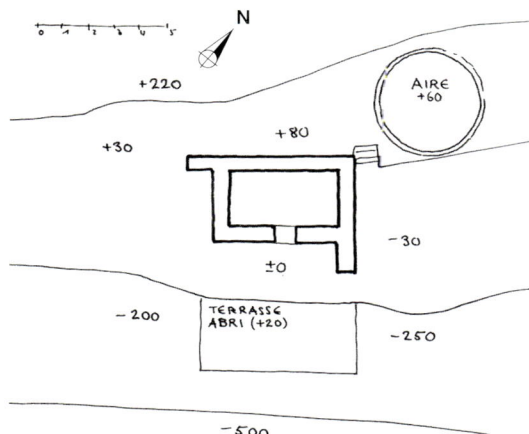

South-west facade

Even higher up, the main valley continues south to the village of XYNARA and Exomvourgo, the mountain summit and the ancient citadel of the island. To its left, a small valley ascends to Krokos and Loutra, where the Ursulines have their monastery. To its right, another small valley ascends in the direction of Smardakito. An old, imposing dovecote (56) is located below the village of **SMARDAKITO**, in the fields, near a threshing floor for wheat and a shelter for the neighbouring flocks and herds.

It is roofed with beams and slabs, themselves covered by a layer of clay soil: it seems that the quarries near the village do not yield large slate slabs. On the northwest facade, an open-air staircase gives access to the roof. This dovecote is completely plastered. Like a few other rare dovecotes in the area, it has strange columns in its corners. The cypress is absent from the decoration, which consists exclusively of rhombi and a few suns (see also Fig. 27, p. 102).

South-east facade

57 SMARDAKITO

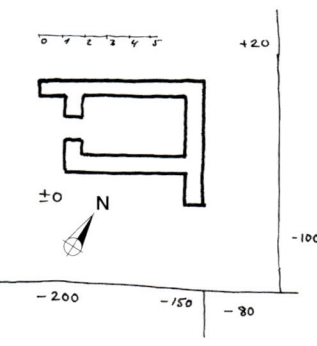

High above **SMARDAKITO**, just an hour's distance away from Tarambados and the ridge that separates the northern part of the island from the south, stands a very nice, old dovecote (**57**), whose decoration consists almost exclusively of carefully placed rhombi. The tall banquettes are prominent. The clay terraced roof is also made of slabs, which are supported by beams.

In the narrow valley that ascends in the direction of Exomvourgo, the village of **KROKOS** hosts, opposite the cafe, a very large dovecote (**58**), consisting of two adjoining edifices.
The decoration is very untidy: many protruding slabs (in the form of a cornice), with and without small openings, and a frieze with triangles, a few suns, a cypress. It is, as a whole, not a very attractive building.

KROKOS 58

59 XYNARA

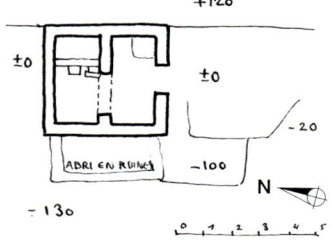

The village of **XYNARA** is located at the foot of Exomvourgo, whose mountain has a large stone cross at the top. The village is the most important in all of Messaria, the seat of the Diocese; it is surrounded by many old dovecotes. One of them (**59**), above the village, is abandoned. At the ground floor there is a wine press and, on the other side of the arch that separates the space, a corner fireplace. The decoration is very symmetrical: in the upper zone of the south side there is a frieze consisting exclusively of suns.

XYNARA **60**

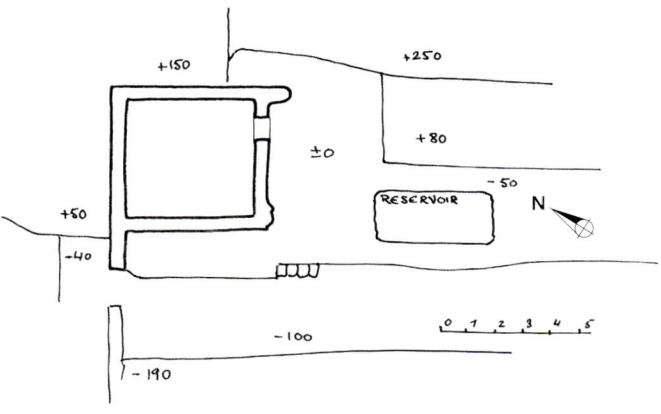

Quite close by, another dovecote (**60**) is characterized by its rounded anta wall, as is visible in the drawing, and also a moulded corner, between the two main facades. It is decorated with great care, with alternating suns and cypresses. Two small stone-built bases support the banquette.

29

THIRD ROUTE

FROM THE PLATEAU OF STENI TO THE TOWN OF TINOS AND THE SOUTHEAST PART OF THE ISLAND

In the centre of the ANO MERI, east of the peak of Exomvourgo, the upland plateau of STENI consists of a large, fertile, cultivated plain, surrounded by many villages. The most important of them, Steni, gives its name to the whole plateau. From the plateau, four main valleys descend to the sea:
• To the north, the wide valley of Perastra, by which we ascended from KATO MERI to Exomvourgo.
• To the northeast, a large valley, cut by the Livada river, descends to the bay of the same name.
• To the southeast, a valley, Potamos ton Angellon (the River of Angels), meets the east coast of the island, at Tarsanas.
• In the south, a large valley descends in the direction of the town of Tinos and the Bay of Agkali.
Between the last two valleys, which are separated by the plain of Steni and Mount Kechrovouni, lies the village of Arnados that dominates two more small valleys, which descend to the sea. In one of them, southeast of Triantaros, there is a nice dovecote (82), near the area of Kounares. Further west, the most important small valley of Passavas descends from the village of Triantaros to the sea, passing by the chapel of Agia Marina.
Let us traverse these valleys, seeking out their dovecotes.

29. The rough cobbled path (*kalderimi*) running in the direction of the plateau of Steni.

30. The lace-like dovecote converses with the imposing mountain mass of Exomvourgo, while the stepped terraces with their crops lie between them.

31. This beautiful dovecote, now reduced to ruins, was located south of the old Venetian castle of Exomvourgo, which dominates the whole island from its height of 641 meters above sea level.

32. The interior of the castle of Exomvourgo with its prehistoric cyclopean walls.
33. Small square in the centre of the picturesque village of Triantaros.
34. Covered alleyway in the village of Triantaros.
35. Between the port of Tinos (Chora) and the village of Tarambados, at the edge of a small valley, stands this truly beautiful dovecote (75). It is still whitewashed and its decoration is perfectly symmetrical. The banquettes are set on stone-built bases.

61 FALATADOS

The first valley starts, heading northeast, below the village of **FALATADOS**, which is almost as big as Steni. Very close by, on the side opposite the village, above the natural basins where the women washed clothes the night I passed by, is the dovecote of Annoula Kolarou (**61**).

It is an old dovecote, decorated with great care, mainly with rhombi and herringbones, rare motifs in this area. Also noteworthy are the cypresses of various types. One of the banquettes is made up from two narrow stone-built bases. The upper frieze does not really have openings, but a few exist in the rhombi. The skilfully made decoration of the anta wall is of particular interest.

FALATADOS **62**

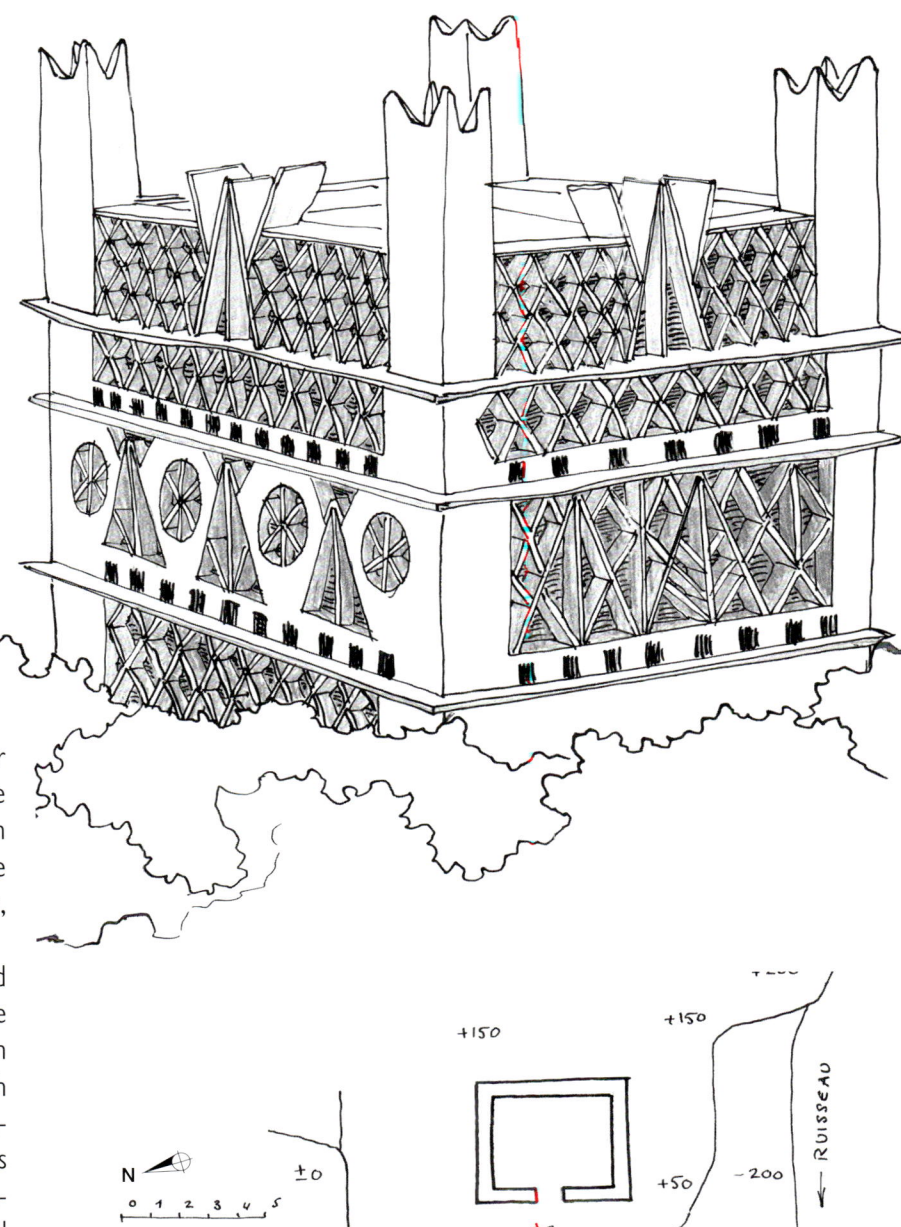

The northern slope of the valley is steep. Lower down, the other side is cultivated and there are some dovecotes. One of them (**62**) dominates an olive grove in the small side valley. A large pine tree partially hides it. It is old, in poor condition, but still occupied by pigeons.

The banquettes, in a rare style, are embedded deep into the last frieze with the rhombi. Some of the last are perforated so that the pigeons can pass through. Above there is a narrow frieze with rhombi and small openings. Below, there is another frieze with alternating suns and cypresses, as well as a very interesting composition, which combines rhombi and some strange cypresses. The tall corner posts look even taller than usual as they rise from the highest protruding slab or *liastra*.

Seeing no other dovecotes below, I decided to go back.

63 POTAMIA

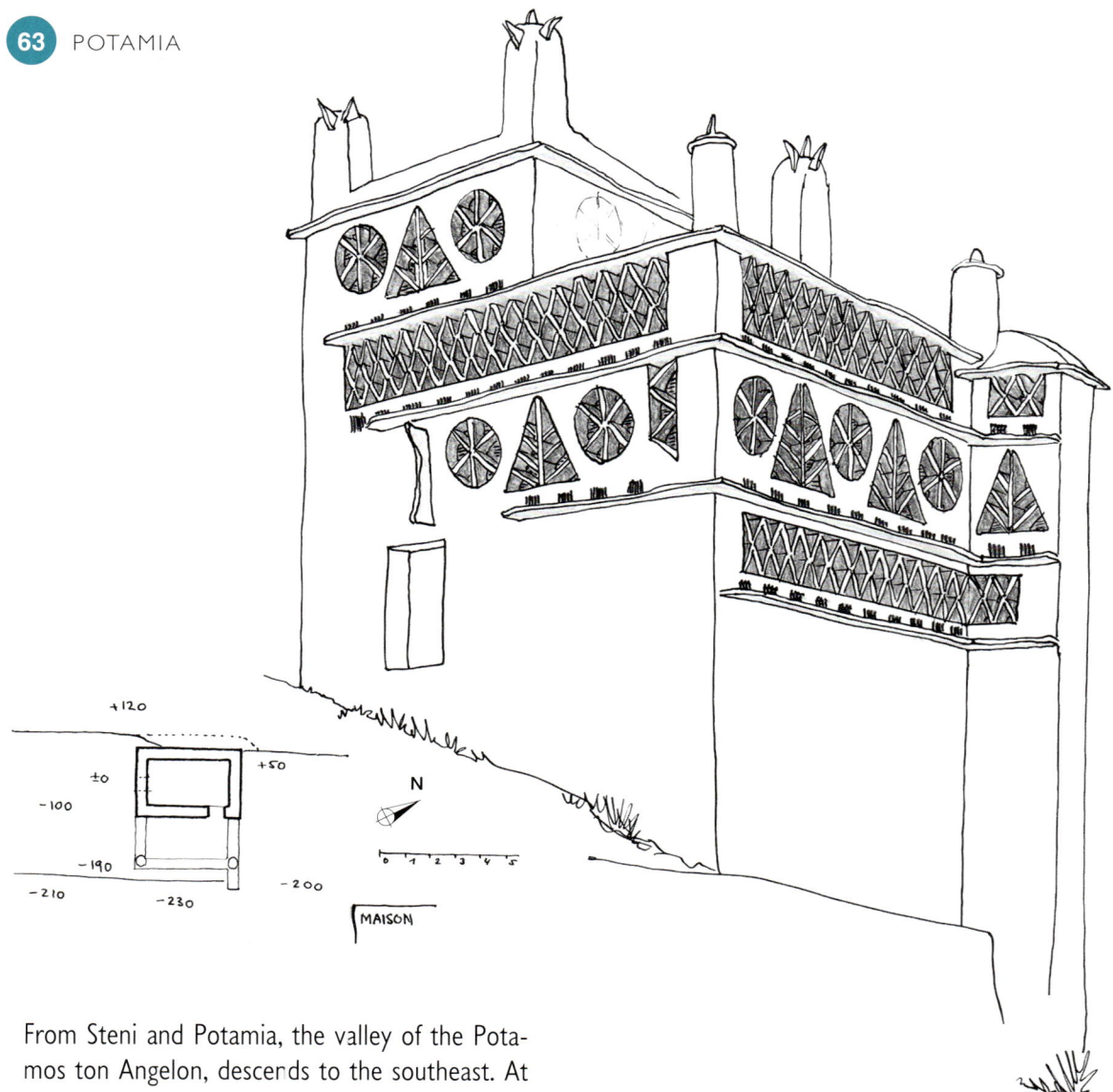

From Steni and Potamia, the valley of the Potamos ton Angelon, descends to the southeast. At dusk when I arrived at the **POTAMIA**, the cafenion owner welcomed me politely and offered me his bed. When he went down to play cards, I took the opportunity and lay down on the blanket he had laid out for himself to sleep on. In the morning, he did not complain much that I left him his own bed. Potamia is a large village; its cobbled streets have many fountains. Above the village, the valley widens and forms a large bowl with many dovecotes.

The dovecote of Maria Giannisopoulou (**63**), built above the last houses of the village, is richly decorated, with interchanging friezes of slabs and ones where suns and cypresses alternate. Pigeons occupy the entire interior. There is access to the upper part from the terraced roof.

POTAMIA 64

A little above the previous one, a nice dovecote rises (**64**). It belongs to Markos Palamaris, who, as I was told, owns half a dozen dovecotes, whose occupants plunder the surrounding fields. This dovecote is old, covered with slabs resting on the internal beams, which are held in place by an arch set in the middle. In 1955, the roofs were cemented. In the stepped anta wall there is a staircase that leads to the upper terrace. The decoration is extremely simple, with rhombi. A series of small openings allow pigeons to pass directly to the front of the building.

65 VALLEY OF KLONAROU

Below, in the valley of the Potamos ton Angelon, the small side valley of Klonarou hosts an old dovecote (**65**), built exclusively from the marble of a small neighbouring quarry. It is in excellent condition, still plastered. The decoration is simple, with austere, clean lines: a frieze with rhombi, and on top of it one with cypresses of different types, on the main facade.

VALLEY OF AKERATOS **66**

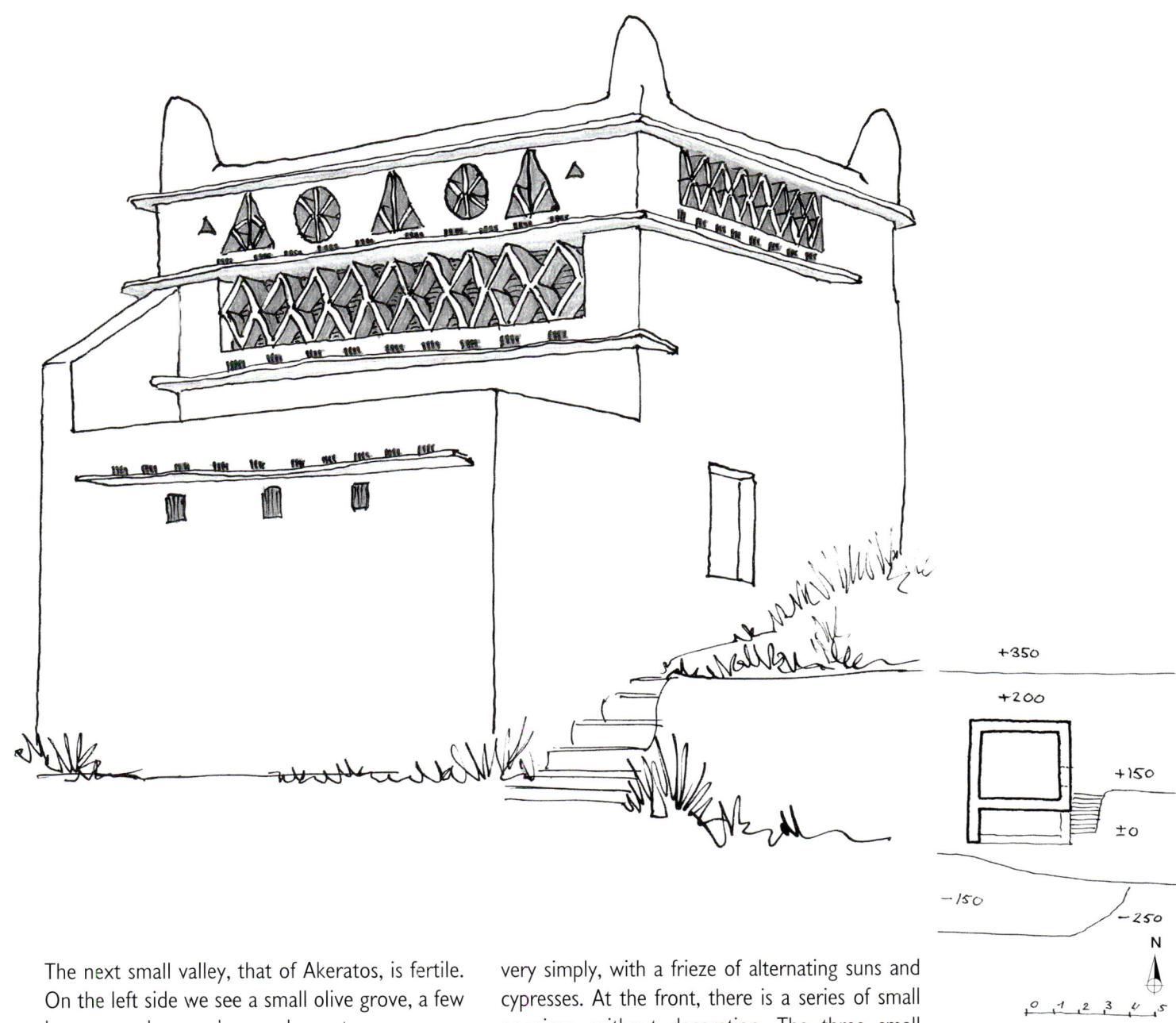

The next small valley, that of Akeratos, is fertile. On the left side we see a small olive grove, a few houses, gardens, and many dovecotes.
One of them, old and beautiful, belongs to a resident of the village of Kechros (**66**). It is decorated very simply, with a frieze of alternating suns and cypresses. At the front, there is a series of small openings, without decoration. The three small openings below were originally used for scaffolding during the building of the wall and then closed off.

67 VALLEY OF AKERATOS

KARYA is one of the most important villages that surround the Steni plateau on the south. From here we will follow the large valley that reaches the sea, in the bay of Agkali, east of the port of Tinos.
Built on a slope, Karya descends into the ravine, where its water-source is located. It commands a valley with many dovecotes.

A little further than the previous one, there is a wonderful, very old dovecote (**67**). It is built of green and brown slate, but some of its plaster has fallen off. Open on two sides, it is extended on the side by an anta wall: the upper frieze of one facade is set a little further back. The decoration is damaged in places, but that of the anta wall, extremely rich, is intact. It very freely combines rhombi, suns and cypresses. The columns show interesting variations.

One of the dovecotes, on the opposite bank, belongs to Giannis Smyros (**68**). Old, plastered and in good condition, it is richly decorated with rhombi, suns and cypresses. The corners are fashioned in a remarkable way: with a corner cypress or a stone carving. A carved marble slab under the banquette lights up the upper floor. An unusual form of banquet with uprights rests on top. There are birds carved on the columns. The eastern retaining wall widens at its base, with two successive internal protrusions of 30 and 35 cm, at 1.50 m and 2.50 m from the ground, respectively.

KARYA 68

69 BELOW SKALADOS

From here, a small valley climbs even higher, almost to the foot of Exomvourgo. Below the village of **SKALADOS** we meet an old, abandoned dovecote, whose roof has collapsed (**69**). It is another example of those dovecotes built around a spring: babbling water flows into the back of a small vaulted portico and is collected in a large tank. A few more tall stone pillars stand around the tank. Below the spring, there is a garden with fencing for the flocks, an indoor shelter, and the dovecote.

VANI 70

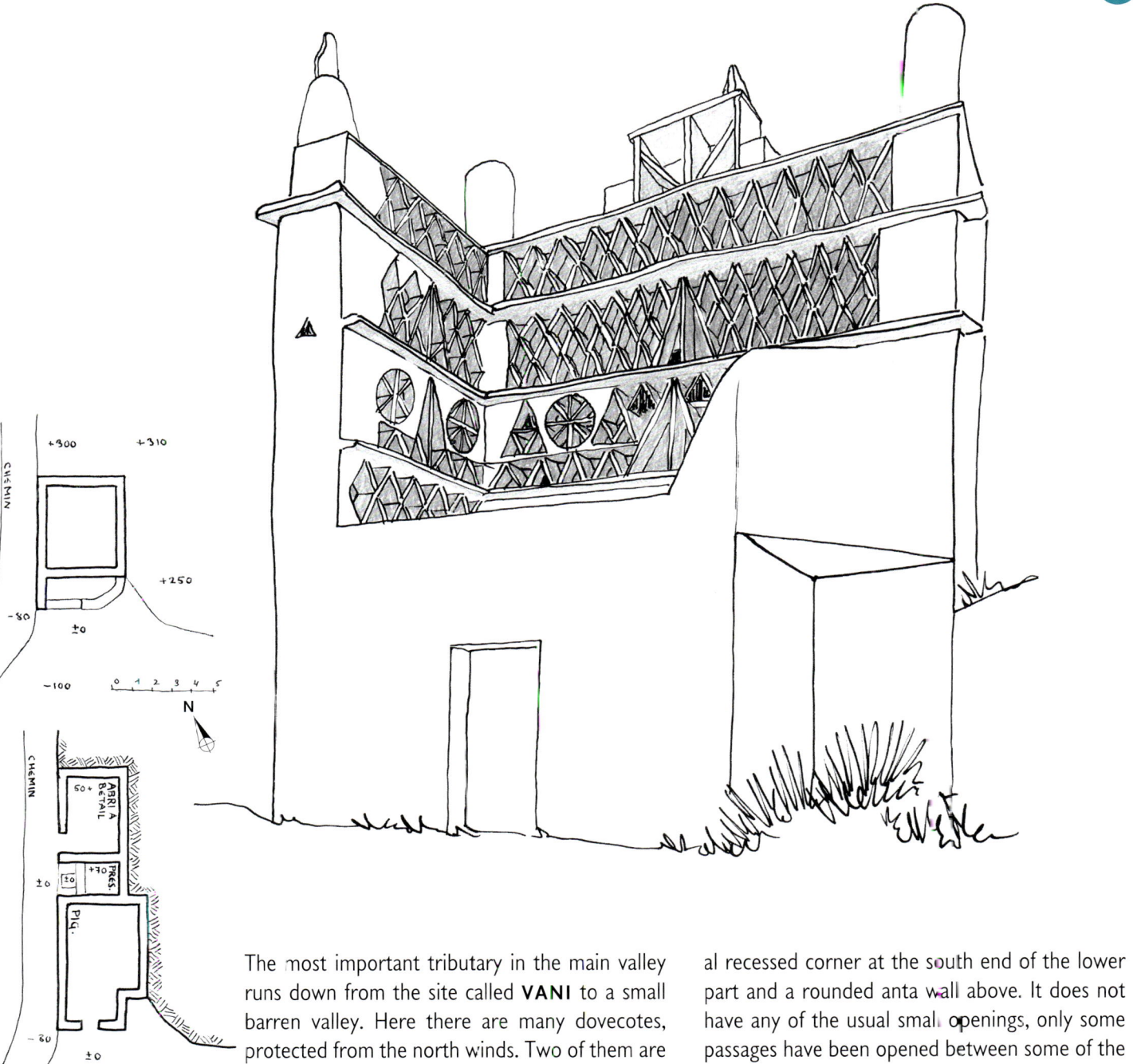

The most important tributary in the main valley runs down from the site called **VANI** to a small barren valley. Here there are many dovecotes, protected from the north winds. Two of them are of particular interest. The first is old (**70**), but still plastered and whitewashed, though abandoned. Built on the edge of a small path, it has an unusual recessed corner at the south end of the lower part and a rounded anta wall above. It does not have any of the usual small openings, only some passages have been opened between some of the decorative slabs.
An animal shelter and a wine-press, their low ceilings covered with long slate slabs, lead to the path.

71 VANI

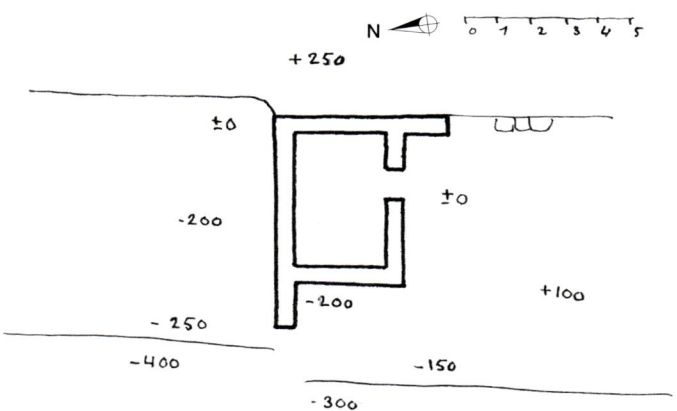

The other dovecote (**71**) has small solid masses of marble in its stonework, but its slabs are made of slate. Richly decorated, it presents the well-known pattern of alternation: a frieze of rhombi, the next with suns and cypresses, and then again a frieze with rhombi. The decoration extends everywhere, even up to the anta walls.

This dovecote is currently in use and in excellent condition. Its roof is cemented and although some plaster has fallen off, it is whitewashed. Finally, one of the columns, equipped with two small niches, somewhat resembles a chimney.

72 BETWEEN VANI AND THE TOWN OF TINOS

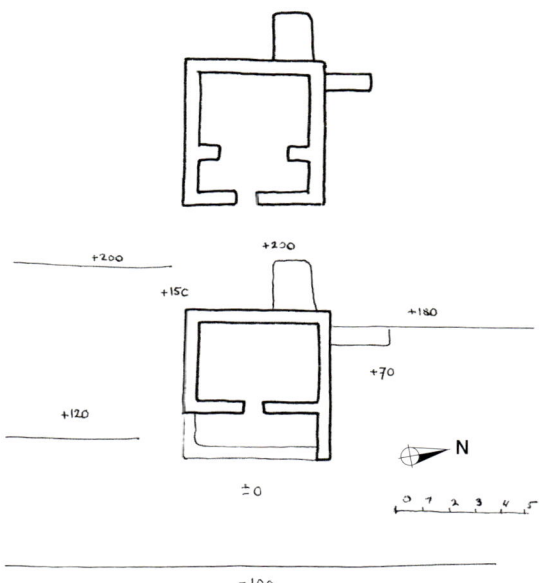

Approaching the coast, the slopes of the main valley widen, revealing beautiful olive groves and gardens. Of the numerous dovecotes established in the area, few are of any interest.

But an old, large dovecote (**72**) rises among the olive trees. The ground floor is used to stack straw. Access to the dovecote is through a small door that leads to the front terrace. The roof is made of slabs supported by beams. Amongst the very rich decoration, in addition to the usual patterns, a decorative element somewhere between the sun and the cypress, in the shape of a clam, is used. The composition of the friezes holds surprises: a series of small openings between two cornices, or cypresses that spread from one frieze into another. The dovecote is plastered, but two stone walls had to be erected to support the northeast corner which was in danger of collapsing.

73 AGIA TRIADA

A small river, Rassonas, flows towards the bay of Agkali, with a ridge, Kechrovouni, separating it from the upland plateau of Steni. For a change, we will climb once more up this valley from the monastery of Agia Triada, located very close to the sea, to the villages of Triantaros and Arnados. There are no more monks in the monastery. I meet an old security guard, who poured me coffee and showed me the ancient marbles that have been built into the walls. Many dovecotes are erected around the monastery, and several of them are relatively recent.

Alexandros Koufakis is the owner of an old, plastered dovecote (**73**). We may note the simplicity of its decoration and the elegance with which two cypress trees are surrounded by slabs, framing a sun in the centre. We also note the anta wall, which extends to the north wall.

AGIA TRIADA, **74**

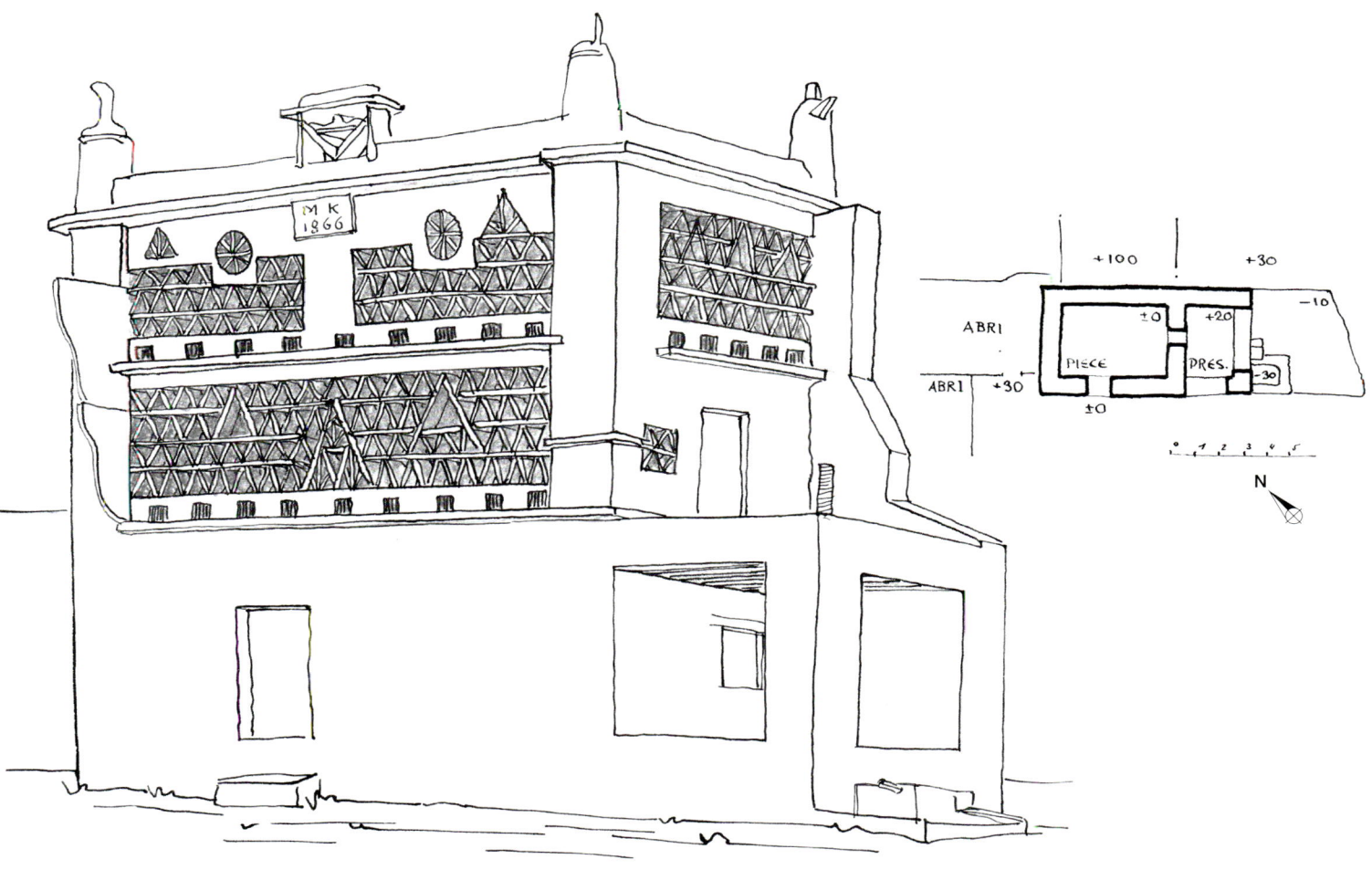

Very close to this is the dovecote of Markos Kritikos (**74**), which is even more interesting. Plastered and whitewashed, it is in excellent condition. It adjoins some relatively low animal shelters, and a small carved slab bears the year of its construction: 1866. At the ground floor level there is a room, independent of the dovecote. The front part is occupied by a wine press, with a large opening to the outside. The must flows into a small basin dug into the ground. In the press, above the pillar in the corner, stands a thin marble column, with finely carved volutes which could be ancient. The decoration is very fanciful in its overall composition, with an original cypress tree in the lower frieze and a small decorated square next to the entrance. Also noteworthy is the unexpected shape of the anta wall, as well as the protruding vertical slabs at the edge of the decoration of the main facade.

75 PRIASTRO

Although it is quite narrow, the valley of **PRIASTRO** supports in its depths a large cluster of olive trees. In the middle, near the church of the Holy Cross, the children collected olives. The valley has many side-branches. Dozens of old dovecotes arise on every side.

The most beautiful dovecote belonging to Petros Vidalis from Mountados (**75**) rises up on the west side of the small side valley, above the olive trees, and is surrounded by a few fig trees. Its decoration, although one common enough in the area, is made with remarkable confidence and delicacy: a frieze with rhombi, one with suns and cypresses above it, and another with rhombi again. As elsewhere in the centre of the island, the usual corner columns have been replaced by tall square pillars.

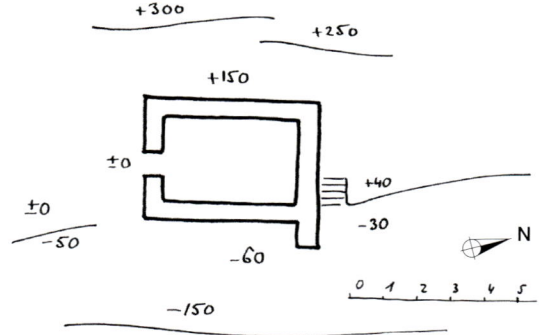

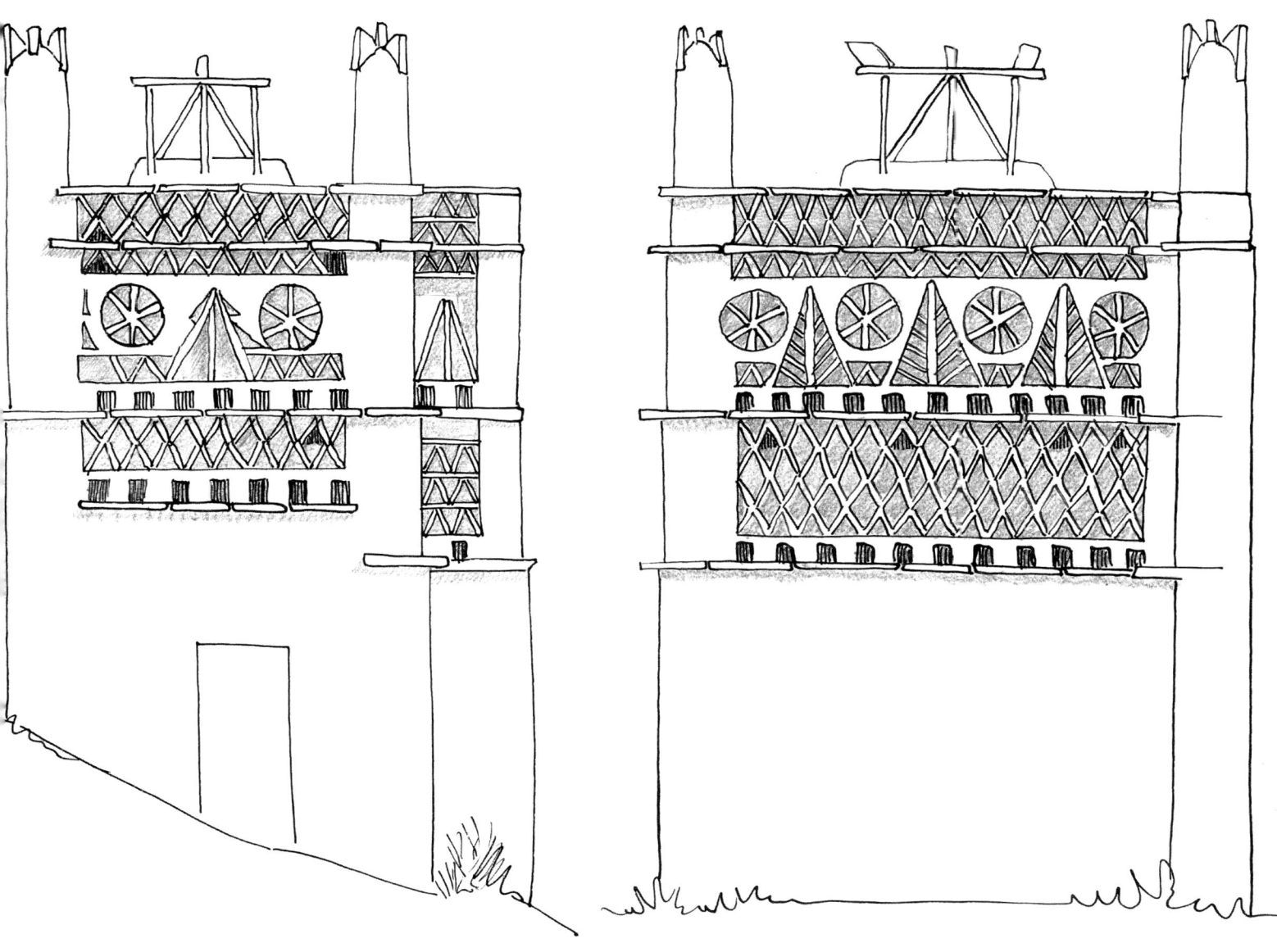

South facade

East facade

161

76 PRIASTRO

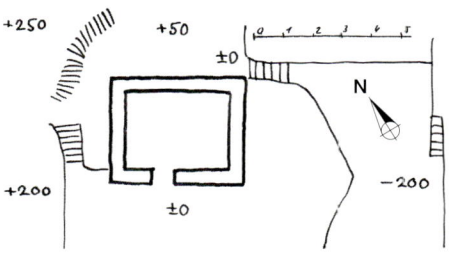

On the right bank of the torrent, above a small olive grove, an old dovecote, partially plastered, belongs to Panagiotis Desypris (**76**). As in the previous one, only rhombi are used in the lower and topmost friezes. The intermediate frieze is decorated exclusively with suns. There are tall square pillars at the ends of the crowning, and a cypress in the corner.

TRIANTAROS 77

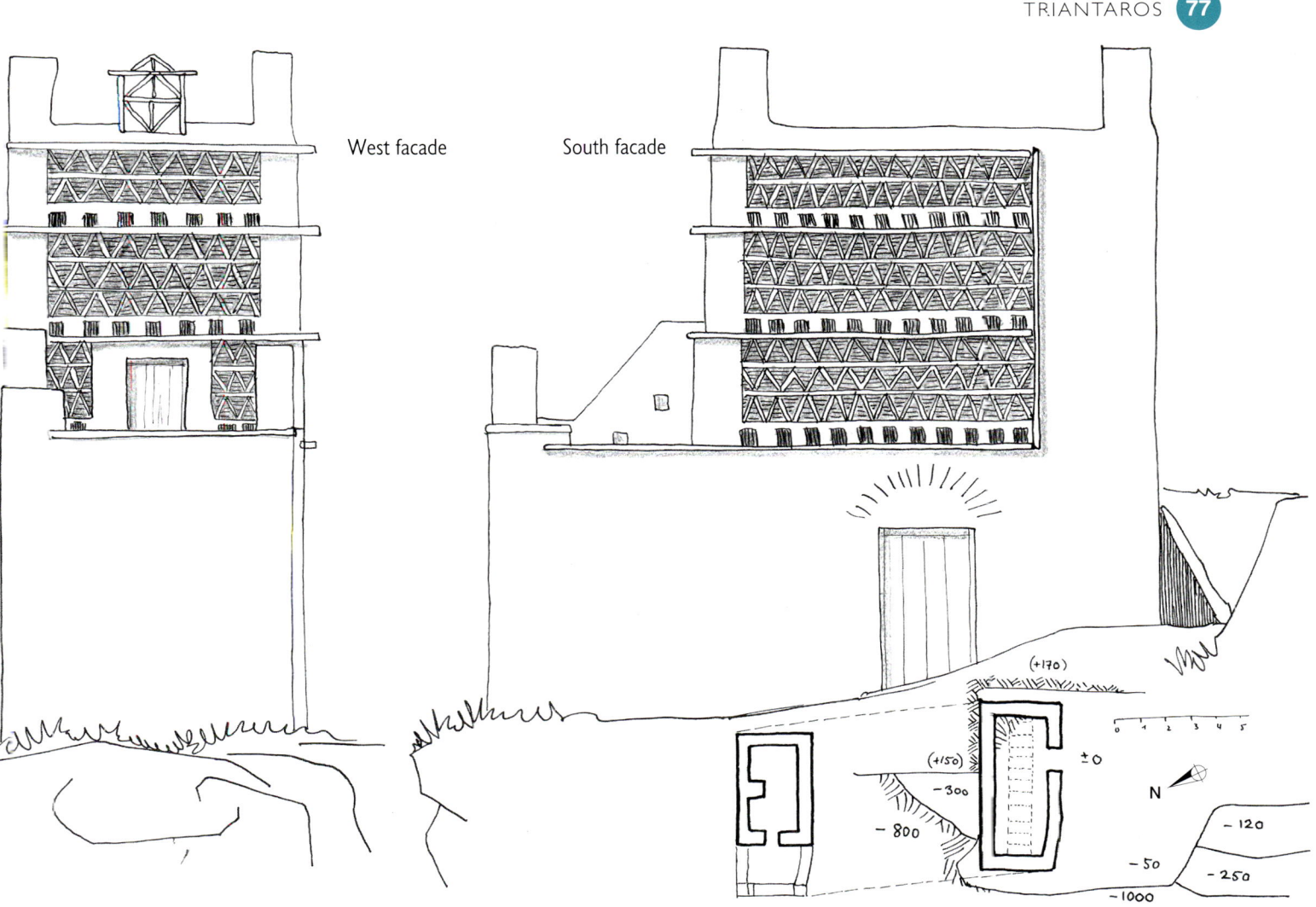

West facade South facade

In a small valley that descends from a spring at **TRIANTAROS**, there is an old, narrow dovecote, which is still plastered (**77**). At the ground floor there is a shelter covered with large slabs placed on the protruding walls. A type of tunnel, consisting of sloping slabs, provides effective protection against ground moisture. The entrance of the dovecote is on the terraced roof. It is also covered with slabs, but because the ledge is small, they had to build a stone wall supporting two slabs, parallel to their long sides, on which perpendicular slabs rest. We also notice the design of the banquette and the small plaque on the east wall: "M. K". The owner, Petros Kardamitzis, from Triantaros, has died, and the dovecote house now belongs to his wife, Katerina.

78 TRIANTAROS

Behind the previous example, on the right bank of the stream, there is a nice old dovecote that belongs to Andreas Palapatis, from Triantaros (**78**). It is raised at the flank of an olive grove, and is protected from ground moisture by a semicircular ditch and not by a tunnel, like the previous ones. Its decoration consists of two decorative friezes: in the lower there is a door. The decoration of the upper frieze is very free-styled, it focuses on a cypress and two suns.

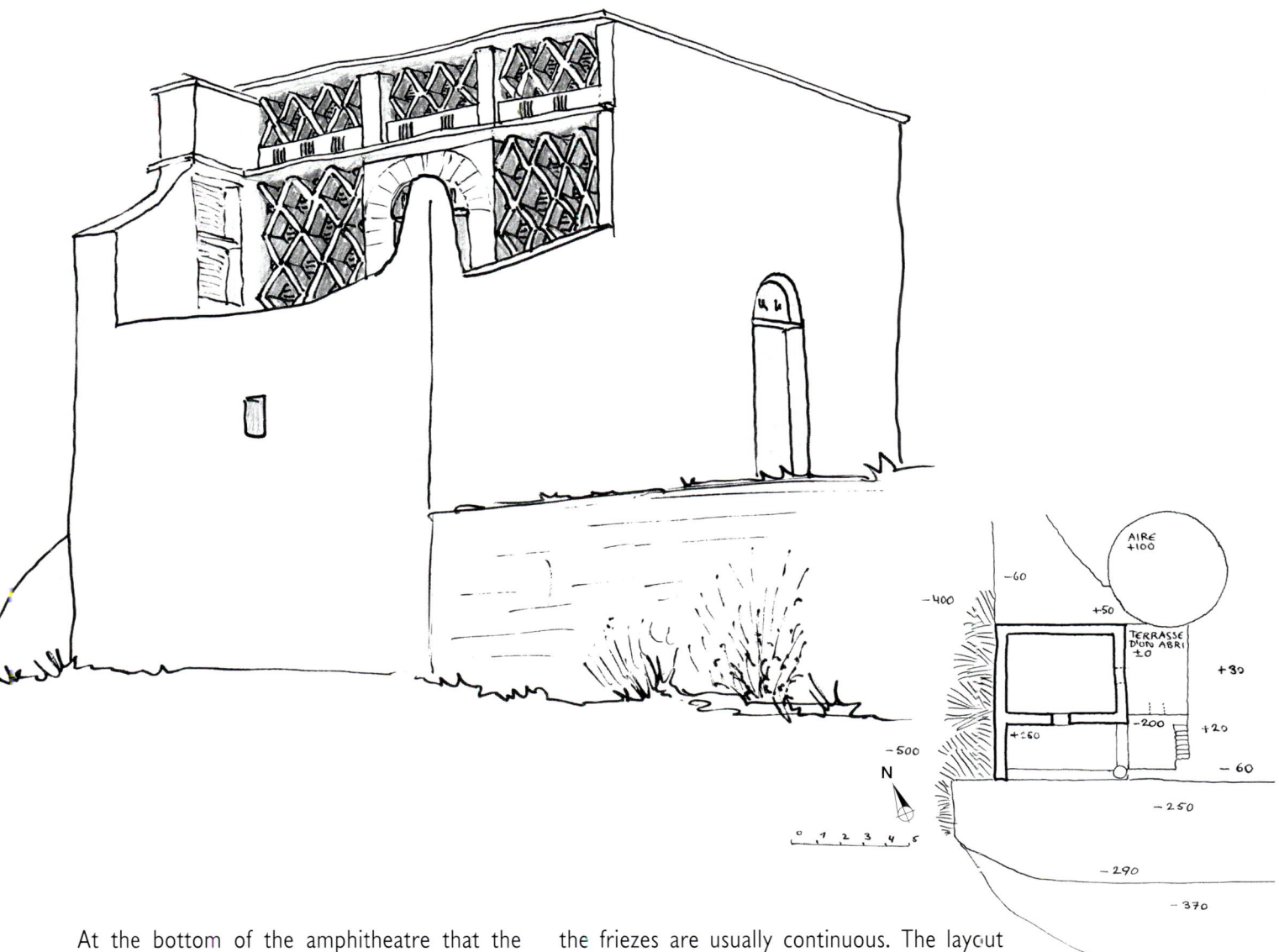

At the bottom of the amphitheatre that the valley forms, between the olive trees and the lemon groves, is an old dovecote dating from April 1852. A little higher up, we encounter another old dovecote whose plaster has almost fallen off, which belongs to Antonios Louvaris (**79**). It has a style quite rare in the area, where the friezes are usually continuous. The layout used here is due to the existence of a door on the terrace, which divides the upper frieze into three parts. A small staircase leads to a small courtyard, which gives access to a covered area. There they stack the straw, and then press it in a neighbouring area.

80 TRIANTAROS

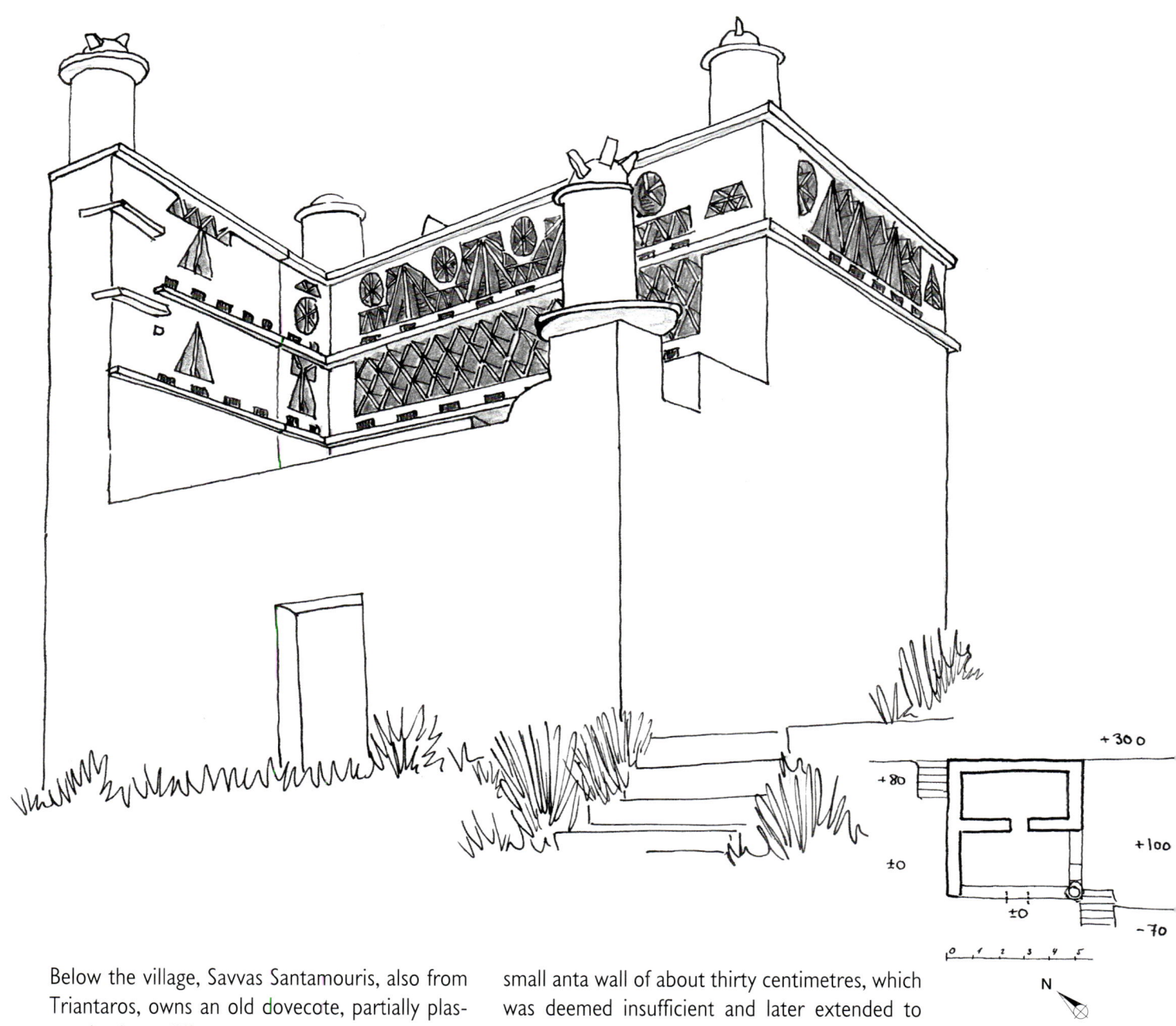

Below the village, Savvas Santamouris, also from Triantaros, owns an old dovecote, partially plastered, whose different volumes are yet in harmonious balance (**80**). The entrance of the dovecote is on the front terraced roof. Initially it had only a small anta wall of about thirty centimetres, which was deemed insufficient and later extended to the edge of the roof. A massive column, crowned with a stone hemisphere, balances skilfully the anta wall.

NEAR TO BERDEMIAROS 81

Having rushed at speed from below **TRIANTAROS**, from one dovecote to another, I arrived at night in the village cafe. The kind villagers offered me something to eat. I slept comfortably on a mattress. The next morning, I ate again and of course, when it was time to leave the village, these people refused to let me give them anything. Nevertheless, because it is a cafe, I put a note under an ashtray. In a small side valley, in the direction of **BERDEMIAROS**, is to be found the beautiful dovecote of Antonios Kardamitsis (**81**). The access to it is peculiar: a tiny door (65 by 80 cm), placed three meters from the ground, opens into the first floor. To get there, you have to climb up to the terraced roof, on which the dovecote rests (+1,80), and then put your feet in the two small niches near the door. This dovecote is still sufficiently well plastered and completely whitewashed.

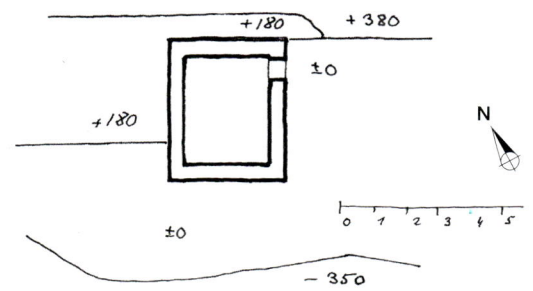

82 KOUNARES

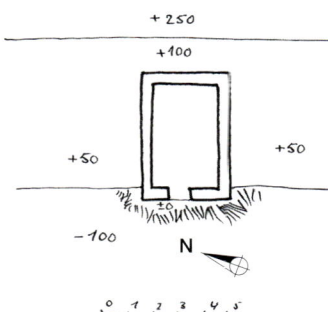

In the last, almost uninhabited, small valley, which is located between the valleys of Triantaros and Potamia and hosts many dovecotes, rises a small one (**82**) in the location of **KOUNARES**. It is another example of the local style, with three decorated friezes and three very high corner posts. Its dimensions are impressive: the main facade, facing, is extremely narrow, and when you see it from below it looks like a tall tower.

EAST OF THE TOWN OF TINOS **83**

We will complete these walks with a description of some dovecotes in the town of Tinos. To the east of the town, after passing the last houses, we quickly arrive at a large, almost uncultivated plain, which extends to the sea. On the left side of the road, we see hills rising up, scattered with dovecotes. Among them, is an old dovecote of large dimensions, richly decorated, with its plaster almost intact (**83**).

Made of slate, like all dovecotes in the area, it has a rare feature: almost all rhombi are made of small bricks instead of slabs. We also notice the small central motif in the shape of a coat-of-arms, and the stone wall placed on the banquette, to enhance its resistance to the wind.

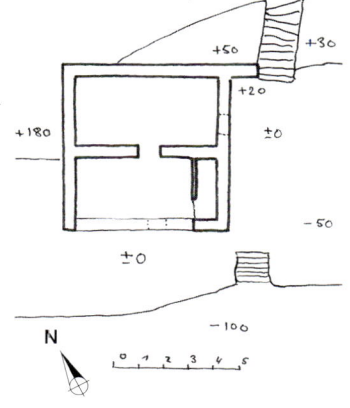

169

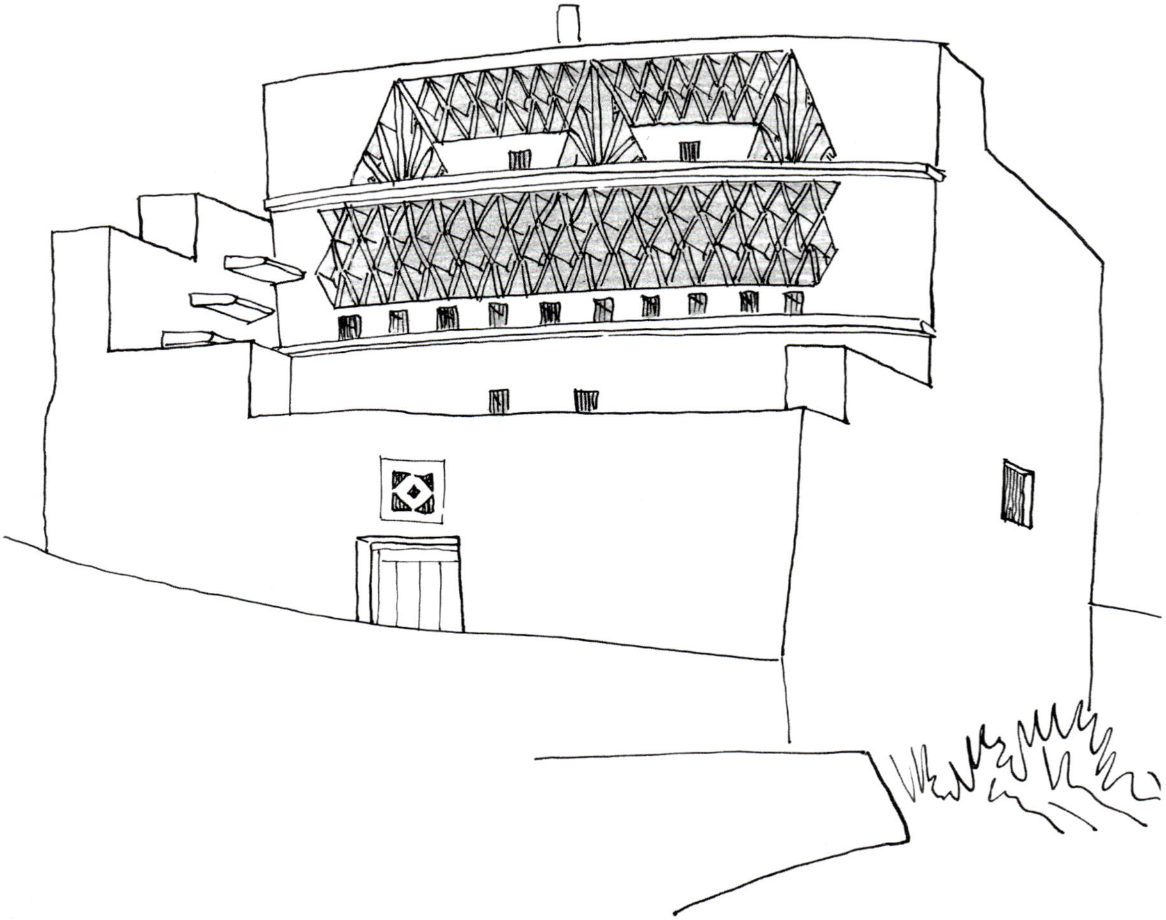

84 ELLINOPI

A small valley, named **ELLINOPI**, comes to its end northwest of the city. Although barren, it has a few trees on its western slope. From the bed of the ravine begins a path, which soon ends in groves of oleanders and brambles.

On the right side of the valley, next to a few olive trees, rises a nice, old dovecote (**84**), owned by Giorgos Siotis, who lives in Tripotamos. It has many interesting features: the slightly arched shape of the front or the stepped shape of the anta wall, where some cantilevered slabs facilitate access to the roof.

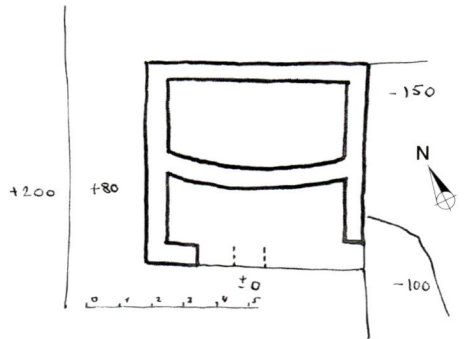

ELLINOPI 85

Higher up, the small valley widens and is again covered by trees and gardens. An old dovecote, which rests on two animal shelters, belongs to a resident of Smardakito (**85**). Sometimes, an inherited dovecote lies very far afield from its owner. Its L-shaped form is quite rare. Its decoration has a very clever layout, as it plays on the alternation of two types of cypresses and covers the gaps between them with small triangular patterns. Next to the west facade is the threshing floor, where the wheat is processed, surrounded by a series of slate slabs.

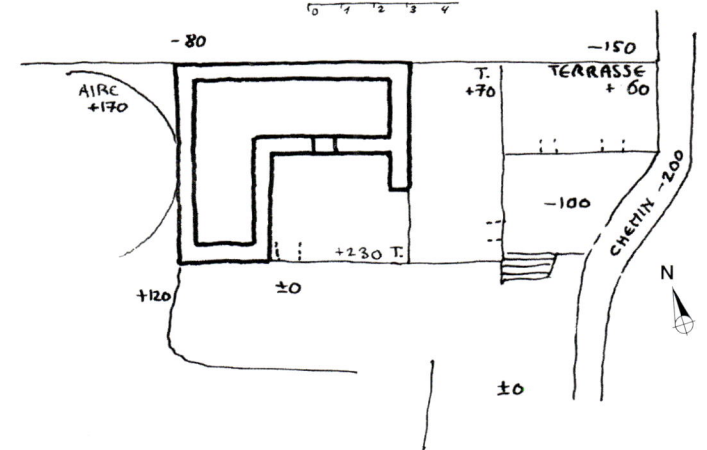

CONVERSION OF WINDMILLS INTO DOVECOTES

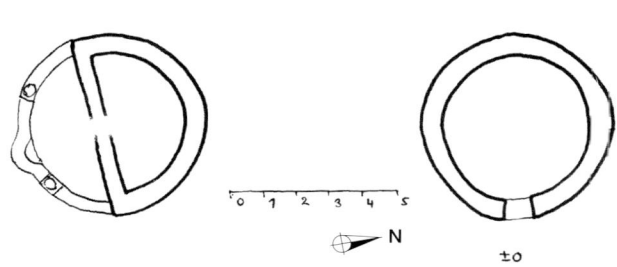

And to get away from all these dovecotes, we will stop presenting them here, while we continue to remain in the town of Tinos, with a description of two old windmills. However, both these well-built windmills stopped operating at some point and became... dovecotes!

I counted three on the outskirts of the town. One of them, fully plastered, belongs to Stelios Vlachakis (**86**). The walls of the old mill were preserved throughout the height of the ground floor, and above that a facade was made with a diametrical trough on top, through which the pigeons could enter.

All the traditional elements were observed: horizontal slabs (cornice?), rows of small openings, decoration (in this case, but elementary), banquettes and columns. There are, in fact, in the front of the construction two small columns, reminiscent of those that exist at every corners of the dovecotes.

The very tall, old mill (**87**) pictured on pages 174–175 presents a rather complex arrangement. The old spiral staircase, which rests on a thick cutting of the outer wall, has been preserved and supports the facade of the dovecote. The staircase then leads through a small door to the upper flat roof, five meters above the ground. Because the wall is very thick, they did not make small openings in the upper part of the decoration. Only a few small openings lower down allow access to the dovecote, which is not separated by any intermediate floor. The building is plastered and belongs to Afentoulis, a physician from Tinos.

TOWN OF TINOS 86

87 TOWN OF TINOS

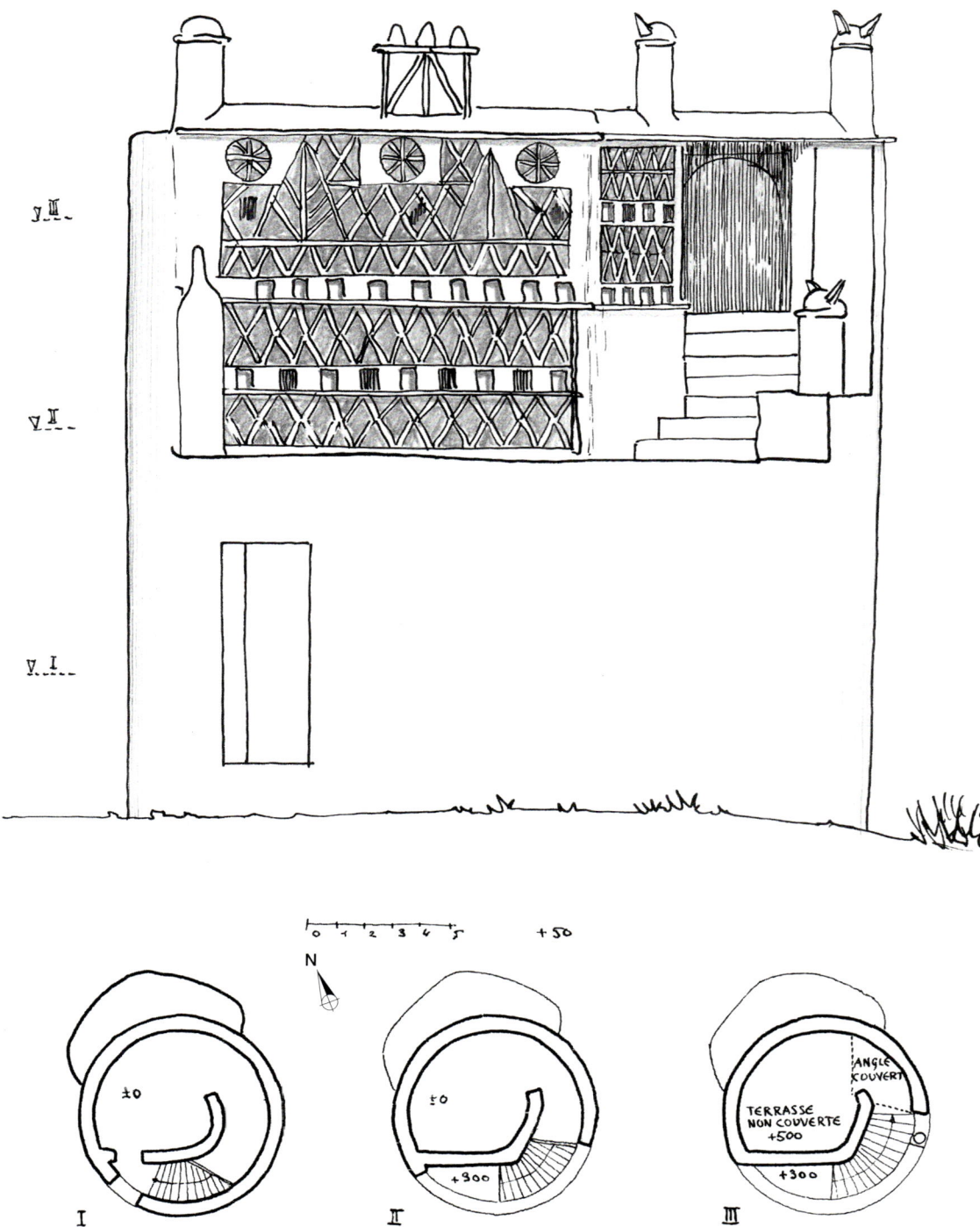

Here ends the account and the tour in the island of the dovecotes.
A summary of the unpublished 4-volume study made in 1955 for the dovecotes of Tinos,
presented at the Geneva School of Architecture by Manuel Baud-Bovy.
Athens – Geneva – Volos 2021

SELECTED BIBLIOGRAPHY

Οι περιστεριώνες της Τήνου — πλήρης καταγραφή, (photo album), Manthos Prelorentzos, (Private Edition, 2020).
Τήνος, Περιστεριώνες (photo album), Aristeides Karagiorgis, (Athenian Brotherhood of Teniots, 2016).
Mediterranes Ökosystem / Kultur und Naturlandschaften der Griechischen Insel Tinos, Hasso Hohmann, 2011.
Ανεξερεύνητη Τήνος (travel guide), Vali Vaimaki, Road Publications, Athens 2005.
Τήνος: 12 περιστεριώνες (album with paintings), Iosif V. Hatzipaules, Philipotes Publications, 1996.
«Peristeriones - Eine Architektur nicht für Menschen gemacht?», Kosta Mathéy, *Trialog* 42 (1994), 42–51.
Περιστερεώνες της Τήνου, D. Vallianos & D. Vokos, Philipotes Publications, 1986.
Τήνος, Aggeliki Haritonidou, 1983, offprint from the 8-volume work *Greek Traditional Architecture*, Melissa Publications.
Περιστεριώνες στην Τήνο και την Άνδρο, Dolly Goulandris, Museum of Cycladic Art Publications, 1977.
«Dovecots of Tenos», Manuel Baud-Bovy, *Architecture*, September 1959, vol.17, p. 60–65.

SOURCE OF IMAGES AND DRAWINGS:
All the illustrative material of the book comes from the archive
of the author, unless otherwise stated.

CREATIVE DIRECTOR: **MOSES KAPON**
ARTISTIC DESIGNER: **RACHEL MISDRAHI-KAPON**
COPY EDITOR: **NICHOLAS HAROKOPOS**
DTP: **ELENI VALMA, MINA MANTA**
PROCESSING OF ILLUSTRATIONS: **MICHALIS TZANNETAKIS**